Abraham the Trinity and Lot Exonerated Genesis 18 & 19

This account from the Jewish Torah or
the Hebrew Old Testament proves the
Triune Godhead-Jehovah God
manifested himself to Abraham
as three persons

By Terry Lee Miller Sr.

Eternity Publications
1252 Sessions Road
Elgin, SC 29045
tmgen18@aol.com

This book was printed in the United States of America.

Abraham the Trinity and Lot Exonerated Genesis 18 & 19

Genesis 18 AND 19 contains Hebrew Jewish Old Testament proof that Jehovah God is one Triune God and was manifested as one God in three persons in these chapters.

ALSO...

Chapters 18 and 19 of Genesis totally exonerates and clears Lot from the defamatory false charges from every corner of the world that he was a wicked backslider who deserved shame and disgrace!

Dedication

This book is dedicated to our Jewish friends who, we pray, will recognize the Lord Jesus Christ as their Messiah God and Savior

ISAIAH 9:6

For unto us a child is born, unto us a son is given and the government shall be upon His shoulder and His name shalll be called Wonderful, Counsellor, the Mighty God, the Everlasting Father, the Prince of Peace

ISAIAH 7:14

Therefore the Lord himself shall give you a sign, behold a virgin shall conceive and bear a son and shall call his name Immanuel. (Which being interpreted is 'God with us.')

Abraham the Trinity and Lot Exonerated Genesis 18 & 19

Table of Contents

Introduction

Far too long the forces of Satan have attacked the Scriptural teaching of the Deity of our Lord Jesus Christ. Upon close examination, it can be easily understood that even in fundamental evangelical circles the average Christian is vulnerable to cults, isms, and schisms, who claim that Jesus was nothing more than an archangel, a created being or an angelic spirit in His pre-incarnate state. Fortunate for us is the fact that at least most of the cults (i.e.: Mormons, Watchtower, etc) have basically maintained that Jesus was a pre-incarnate being. This is where we can begin proving who Jesus really is. With others, such as modern Judaism, this book will once and for all prove, from Old Testament Scriptures, that the Lord Jesus Christ was nothing less than one person of the triune Godhead. Jesus is equal with God the Father in every sense. Notice, dozens of O.T. prophecies concerning the coming Jewish Messiah were exactly fulfilled in the Lord Jesus Christ when He came the first time!

Isaiah 7:14, and 9:6.

"Therefore the Lord Himself shall give you a sign. Behold a virgin shall conceive and bear a son and shall call His name Immanuel." " For unto us a child is born, unto us a son is given, and the government shall be upon His shoulder, and His name shall be called Wonderful, Counselor, the mighty God, the everlasting Father, the Prince of Peace."

While Jehovah God is one God, He is also one God manifested in three persons, i.e. the triune God whom we love and serve. Just as water can be manifested as a trinity, water, stream and ice and as well the sun as one sun can be manifested as a trinity, light, heat and chemical energy so with God. God manifested as the Father, the Word/Son and the Holy Spirit. The fact that God is omnipotent (all powerful) draws the firm conclusion that God is not subject to time, space, or to our prejudiced, preconceived ideas, and can manifest Himself when and how He sees fit.

"Interpretation" of Scripture, or any passage of Scripture, can easily destroy the plain meaning of God's Words. This is seen when the Watchtower claims that Luke 16 (the rich man and Lazarus) is not true in itself, but is merely a parable, which supposedly conveys another truth, thus the reader is not to take God's Words literally. However, nowhere did Jesus call Luke 16 a parable! Neither did Luke! All parables in all four Gospels are identified as parables, and are <u>always, true stories in themselves,</u>

drawn from real life occurrences to convey spiritual truths. The Watchtower claims for one to be consciously suffering in a literal place called HELL, would be cruel and unjust. If the claims of the Watchtower are true, then Jesus (whom they claim was holy and righteous) told a lie to convey a truth. To the contrary, our Lord and Savior <u>never</u> lied. Even if this account in Luke 16 were a parable, it takes a truth to tell a truth. and Luke 16 stands true in itself. It means what it says. Luke 16 is a simple warning to the unrighteous of their fate if they will not repent.

The Watchtower also corrupts the Word of God by adding the unwarranted definite article "a" in John 1:1. This makes Jesus "a god," rather than being The God and equal with God."... the Word was with God, and the <u>Word was God</u>." Their position denies the Trinity and the deity of Jesus. [I Jn. 3:1; 5:6-9]. All this heresy easily falls apart by understanding the following: if Jesus were merely "a god" then he would have had to be created by Jehovah God. If created by Jehovah God, then plainly the All-Mighty God <u>created the lesser "god" Jesus.</u>

This heresy is easily exposed by reading a favorite passage the Watchtower quotes in their visitation ministries: (Isaiah 43:10) "Ye are my witnesses, saith the LORD, and my servant whom I have chosen: that ye may know and believe me, and understand that I am he: before me there was no God formed, neither shall there be after me. I am the Lord! And beside me there is no Savior" (continued at Isaiah Chapter 45). See also Hosea 13:4. [Jn. 8:19, 58; 14:6-7].

Search also these verses: Ephesians 5:23: "... even as Christ is the head of the church: and he is the Savior of the body." I Timothy 4:10: "...we trust in the living God, who is the Savior of all men ..." I John 5:20: "... we are in him that is true, even in his Son Jesus Christ. This is the **true God,** and eternal life." I Timothy 3:16: "... God was manifest in the flesh..." The plain teaching is that <u>God came in the flesh!</u> Further identification of Jesus with Jehovah is in Acts:20:28: "Take heed therefore unto yourselves, and to all the flock, over the which the Holy Ghost hath made you overseers, to feed the church of **God**, which **He** hath purchased with **His own blood."**

The basic reason the Watchtower, Muslims, and others have trouble with the Deity of Jesus is because they have misread the Word of God on the Triune God head, (the basic Christian teaching of one God, but one God manifested in three persons) See I Cor. 12:3. While our Jewish friends reject the New Testament, remember the Jews are God's chosen people even though they, as a nation, have yet to come to accept Jesus as their Messiah. This booklet will clearly prove from their Old Testament Scriptures that Jehovah God is a Triune God.

Finally, before we present this truth, we challenge you, the reader, if you are anti-Trinitarian (opposed to the teaching of the Trinity), to refute these Old Testament arguments for the Trinity in Genesis. 18. If you are honest you cannot! Please follow the development of the doctrine of the Trinity in the Hebrew Old Testament. The books of Moses or the books of the Law, known as the Torah and the Pentateuch by the Jews, are considered by Christian, Muslims, and Orthodox Jews to be sacred books inspired by Jehovah God. Again we make the following assertion:

> The following Old Testament study of Genesis 18 will inconvertibly and indisputably prove beyond question that God is not one person in one God but three persons in one, or the blessed Triune God, one God in three persons. It is no wonder that powers of darkness have fought to obscure and diminish the truth of the Trinity in Genesis 18. (Amazingly some in the church have been complicit in this as well!).

It is interesting that among the Christians, with whom I have shared this information, few are willing to readily accept that Genesis Ch 18, in particular, clearly teaches the Trinity. The church has traditionally been taught and falsely so, that the Trinity has not been clearly taught in the O.T. and that the N.T. is mainly responsible to establish it. Two examples as follows: Dr. Peter Connolly's "First Steps in Christian Theology" (Crescendo Publications, Baptist Bible College, Springfield, MO) page 86 top "The idea of God as a Trinity belongs to Christianity alone ..." and on page 91 further states: "..The O.T. does not contain a full revelation of the Trinitarian subsistence of God..."Then Connolly continues,"Dr. Strong points out that no Jewish writer before Christ's coming has succeeded in constructing from them a doctrine of the Trinity. Only to those who bring to them the light of the N.T. revelation do they show their real meaning. (Further quoting Strong) "Our general conclusion with regard to the O.T. intimations must therefore be while they do not by themselves furnish a sufficient basis for the doctrine of the Trinity, they contain the germ of it possibly, used in confirmation of it when its truth is substantially proved from the N.T." Quoting Dr. Matthews (W. R. Matthews, "God in Christian thought", pg 182) Connolly continues. "Thus though there were preparations for the doctrine both in the O.T. and Jewish thought, it is certainly true that Christianity did not inherit a Trinitarian concept of God from Judaism." It is this authors firm assertion to the contrary that Jehovah <u>did indeed</u> firmly establish his Triune Being in blazing revelation of himself incarnate in the Three Personages of his three man anthropomorphic manifestation to Abraham in Genesis 18! This will be proven in the following pages.

PART I

Astounding Jewish/Hebrew Old Testament documentation, proving the plurality of Jehovah or one God, the only one true God, eternally existant as one God in three persons known in the Old Testament as Jehovah, the word, and the Spirit of God known in the New Testament as God the Father, God the son, and God the Holy Spirit.

"ELOHIM"

~yhil{a/ 'elohiym {el-o-heem'}

KJV Genesis 1:1 In the beginning <u>God</u> created the heaven and the earth. 'Elohiym' plural AV - God , god, judge, GOD.

The Hebrew word Elohim is grammatically plural. The prefix "El" is the singular. The Elohim being plural (not singular) plainly makes this verse readable as "In the beginning *They-God* created the heavens and the earth." Here we have the first indication of a <u>number</u> of Creator <u>persons</u> who make up the Godhead and who were involved in creation of heavens and the earth. The Hebrew Torah stands firm here as the inspired word of Jehovah. The false idea that Christians believe in three Gods falls under the following statement:

"Three Gods would mean three independent, self sustaining Gods acting independently of each other, which no Christian believes about Jehovah! All true Christians believe in the Trinity and that God is one God but yet is three distinct persons in perfect unity, harmony and purpose. All are equal in Divinity and of the same exact Divine essence, but in three distinct persons! This is plurality in unity, or three in one. The first verse in the Hebrew Old Testament indicates Jehovah is a plurality in unity."

While the Hebrew word "Elohim" is plural it has been translated in the English as the singular "God", however, in other places the same word is translated in the plural "gods".

Ex:20:2: I am the LORD thy God, which have brought thee out of the land of Egypt, out of the house of bondage, 3: Thou shalt have no other **gods** before me.. Deut: 5:6:

I am the LORD thy God, which brought thee out of the land of Egypt, from the house of bondage. 7: Thou shalt have none other **gods** before me. KJV Exodus 32:4 "

In Genesis 1:26 "And **God** [plural Elohim] said, **Let us make** man **in our image**, **after our likeness** : ..." It is easy to see here the plural Elohim referring to Himself as "us", we", and "our" which are personal pronouns. Both pronouns indicate more than one person. This cannot be refuted! To those who say that God was consulting with angels or other created beings is to add to God's Words. In fact the Scriptures clear up this dispute in verse 27: "So God created man **in his *own* image,** in the image **of God** created he him; male and female created he them." Man was not created in the image of angels or other created beings, no lesser co-creators here!

More plurality is set forward in Genesis 3:22 (after Adam and Eve sinned): "And the **LORD [Jehovah] God [Elohim]** said, Behold, the man is **become as one of us, to know** good and evil. Later when Nimrod begins to build the tower of Babel the Almighty looks down and makes the following statement: Genesis 11:7: "Go to , **let us go down** , and there confound their language. It is evident that God conferred with the other co-existent, co-equal personages within the Godhead. They are to journey to the earth to scatter the wicked by confusing their language. **"Let us"** is further proof that there is more than one personage in the Godhead. God is a compound unity or a plurality in unity. Notice the exact same Scriptural declaration is in Isaiah 6:8: "Also I heard the voice of the **Lord,** saying, **Whom shall I send** and who **will go for us?** Then said I, Here *am* I; send me."

Plainly we can see one God speaking from His plural unity. This could not be angels whom Jehovah was consulting with since angels are not, nor ever have been, represented by prophets, evangelists, or missionaries. The Hebrew word Elohim is plural, not singular! This name is more generally used of God as revealed in Scripture, pertaining to creation and providence.

It is in the plural, so thus indicating the multiple persons of the Godhead. While today the Nation of Israel is living in disbelief of this important fact, still she is a chosen people of God, awaiting redemption. See footnote.[1]

(See Wilson's Old Testament Word Studies, MacDonald Pub.Co., McLean, VA, p.196)

---

1 That the Jews are indeed God's chosen people, and while Israel at least for the time being is living in disbelief of her promised Messiah the Lord Jesus Christ and the triune Godhead, still though as the scriptures say... "And I will bless them that bless thee and curse him that curses thee and in thee shall all families of the earth be blessed" Gen.12:3. That our Jewish friends will come to see the truth of the blessed Triune Godhead is the end to which this booklet is dedicated. The scriptures teach they will one day receive Jesus Christ as their promised Messiah.

PART II
The Jewish Hebrew Shema

The Jewish Shema in "Hebrew" is as follows…Deuteronomy 6:4

"Shema Israel – Adonai Elohenu,
Adonai Echad." Translated this reads….

"Hear O Israel the Lord our God is one Lord."
The English translation here is obscure….

Strongs Hebrew the original, expands the
English translation so Deut 6:4 is as follows:

All who believe the Old Testament is God's Word (Christians, Jews, Muslims, etc.) fully agree that there is only one God. Not a plurality of gods or more than one god. The Jews call Deut. 6:4 the "Shema", or so named as their declaration that idolatry the worship of more than one God other than Jehovah, is forbidden since there is only one God. The founder of Christianity, our Lord Jesus Christ (Jewish by birth), also taught the same truth (Mk. 12:28-29). He taught it as the first and most important commandment. The following points and Old Testament Scriptures clearly prove that Jehovah is a plurality of 3 persons in one, or one God in three persons eternally and perfectly united as one God. The Godhead. Also the following facts will prove that the Jewish Hebrew Torah (Old Testament), *in the original language,* teaches that Jehovah is not one God in one person, but one God in a plurality of persons. Since the Old Testament was originally written in the Hebrew tongue, it is essential to read it.

The Shema in Hebrew shows that Moses taught and believed in the plurality of one God. Note the ending of "Elohenu" is 'nu'. 'Nu' means "our" and this ending denotes that the word "Elohenu" is plural. Rabbi *Simeon ben Jochai*...says"Come, see the mystery of the word *Elohim*. There are three degrees, and every degree by itself alone...and yet, notwithstanding, they all are one, and joined together in one, and are not divided one from another." (Cottage Bible, Vol. 1, Hartford, 1942, p.11) Thus the Hebrew says *Yisrael, Yehowah ,Elohainoo, Yehowah aichod,* "Hear, Israel, Jehovah, our God, is one JEHOVAH." (Cottage Bible, Vol. I, p.241). This could be equated to the motto of the United States: *e pluribus Unum.*

PART III
"ECHAD"

Next we consider the word "Echad." "Echad" means "compound unity" or <u>several</u> or <u>many in one</u>, as would be one cluster of grapes: i.e., *many or more than one in a compound unity (see foot note).* Had the Hebrew word "Yachid" been used, which means one and only one (in one), then the case would have been entirely different. By accepting the Hebrew Scriptural text as it is written, and to allow the written inspired words of Jehovah to formulate what we believe about HIM, we can make no other conclusion.

Notice carefully in the Old Testament Hebrew with the word "Yachid." that the word is never used to denote the <u>oneness of God.</u> The word "Yachid" is used hundreds of times to denote an absolute unity, but never is it used of Jehovah. Some may say that the Jewish Talmud uses it that way, and we agree that certainly is the case, BUT – the Jewish Talmud was written, not by Jehovah, but by a Hebrew scholar named Moses Maimon (no not the Moses of the Bible). Maimon ERRONIOUSLY USED THE HEBREW TERM "YACHID" WHEN

HE WROTE THE TALMUD. Now just who is the final authority? Moses Maimon a Hebrew scholar who made an erroneous translation, or the Moses of the Bible who originally wrote the Hebrew books of the Law under direct inspiration of God? (The Masoretic Hebrew Text)

We must yield to the Scriptures as they were handed down to us in their original languages as the final authority (Psalm12:6-7), There are many instances such as these where the English Versions/Translations need clarification by the original language. When Maimon wrote the Talmud (the Jewish prayer book) to describe the oneness of God he caused vast confusion among other rabbinical literature that was its offspring. (See Footnote)[1].

This author does not believe that Moses Maimon was deliberately trying to mislead anyone. My opinion is that he was merely trying to emphasize that there is only one and only one true and living God to the exclusion of all others. That may or may not be the case, only God knows.

Remember again, NEVER in the Torah, the Pentateuch, do the Scriptures use "Yachid" in reference to the oneness of Jehovah. It is always "Echad" or a plural unity.

---

1 "The Trinity in the O.T." by Morris Zatru, Th.B M.A. published by "The friends of Israel Missionary and Relief Society Inc. 728 Witherspoon Building, Philadelphia, PA.

PART IV
Genesis, Chapters Eighteen and Ninteen

This section is the most powerful, inconvertible and incontestable proof from God's Word that Jehovah God is a Triune God or a plurality in unity. The most damaging evidence condemning all anti-Trinitarian positions of all ages, has been overlooked, misinterpreted, mis-read, and maybe mocked by some "Christian" (yea, even Trinitarian) scholars. This evidence is found in Genesis, Chapters Eighteen and Nineteen. It is no wonder Satan has done so much to repress these two chapters as to their true meanings. To destroy the doctrine of the Trinity is to destroy the doctrine of the Deity of Jesus Christ. Maybe these scholars were parroting what others said in the past. The comments of the commentators, on these two glorious chapters, presents the false notion that <u>God is one person as one God</u> rather than the truth of God being <u>a plurality in unity</u>.

The Trinitarian Doctrine of the Godhead is negated if we refuse to accept the Scriptures as God gave them concerning Himself. We must evaluate the Scriptures at face value rather than accept misleading footnotes in the margins confusing to the reader! Footnotes and comments are to be judged by the Text, not the reverse. Commentators are subject to the flesh and are therefore prone to possible error. You, the reader, (If you reject the Deity of Christ) are not responsible for that which has been handed down to you along the way, but you are responsible for searching the Truth (Acts. 17:11; Pro. 2). You are responsible to acknowledge, embrace, and receive the truths revealed by the Words of God (Elohim).

To reject God's Written Truths is to close the door on eternal salvation. Elohim is who He IS and what He is regardless of what commentators (such as Ryrie & others) have had to say about these passages we are studying in their false, misleading margin footnotes.

Chapter Eighteen

This Chapter of the Word of God can so clearly reveal the truth of the Trinity of God that modern Judaism is suddenly reduced to an untenable and unscriptural theological system demanding to be completely overhauled and shown to be alien to the true Hebrew Judiastic faith! The true Hebrew faith is that faith which embraces the God of the Old Testament in His Triune Being, and sees the Lord Jesus Christ as the second person of the Godhead who came in the flesh as their promised Messiah. Jesus [**309** Yahowshuwaʿ] is the co-equal Savior of the Godhead Elohim. By means of Jesus the Spirit of Elohim (Gen 1:2, 0430-elohiym) has been made available to all mankind (Acts 1:8).]

Are the Jews God's chosen people? Absolutely! Have they been returned to their homeland? Absolutely so! Will their enemies eventually be destroyed and overcome enabling them to regain all of the promised land, receiving their promised Messiah? Absolutely! Are the modern day Jews ready to receive their Messiah? Absolutely not! The theological system they should hold has been gravely damaged by the following:

1. They have been helped in their unbelief of the triune God by uninformed Christian Scholars who down play down the incarnation of the triune Godhead in Genesis 18:2. They have overlooked the truth in the Old Testament that their Messiah would be Jehovah or "God"

come in the flesh, in the form of man. [Job knew enough that he would see his God in the flesh (Job 19:26)]

2. They have overlooked the truth that the Messiah was to be a suffering Messiah. He would be put to death, and later be raised from the dead (Isaiah. 53),

3. They are aware the Christian church teaches that the three men of Genesis 18 were Jehovah and two angels, or Jehovah and three angels manifested as men...

When Genesis 18-19 are closely examined, they clearly reveal that the Triune Godhead did indeed appear to Abraham as he sat in the door of his tent in the heat of the day!

The following arguments we present are so crystal clear that to deny them is to completely discredit Genesis Eighteen, and call God's Word into disrepute. This truth of the incarnate Trinity is not read into chapter 18, but must be taken at face value, by what the Word of God actually says. Christian commentators or scholars who hold the position this author takes are very rare indeed! (That does not mean such writings do not exist)...

Some early Church Fathers have said that Genesis 18 was read once a year on Trinity Sunday. If my memory serves me well, I believe it was an Episcopalian commentary...

Before going into detail in Chapter Eighteen it is essential to comment in some depth on Chapter Nineteen concerning the two (erroneously called/translated) angels and their visit to Sodom and Gomorrah.

Chapter Nineteen

This author previously held the common view that the two "angels" who entered Sodom and Gomorrah were angels or two "created" angelic beings. Lot addressed them with the Hebrew term "adon" which is rarely used of Jehovah, which means, master, sovereign, master/owner or lord, such as lord of a province or as Sarah called Abraham "adon" or lord. The first time was when he met them coming to the gate of Sodom, here he addressed them in the plural..."lords". Later however, he becomes aware that they were indeed "one" in vs.18 when he addressed them as "Lord" singular for the two! Now I am convinced they were actually two members of the Triune God-head. At first Lot did not understand they were two members of the God Head. The fact the A.V. translates them as "angels" in no way excludes them from being two members of the Trinity since the underlying Hebrew for "angels" is "messenger", or one who is "sent of God".

The Lord Jehovah, having 3 distinct personalities, exercised the option of one personality sending the other two down to Sodom to investigate its wickedness. He told Abraham that was His plan, and did so, thus making the two who went down to be called "malek" or "messengers" which also can be translated "angels." Can someone truthfully say that one or two members of the Trinity cannot come, or be sent by others or another member of the Godhead to bring a message or a warning to someone? These two were indeed the two that left Abraham and went on ahead leaving him standing before the Lord as they were the Lord also. All equal essence of Jehovah God! Again, yes the term "angel" is used but that is the English for messengers in Hebrew and Greek. That the two messengers had supernatural powers (1) by smiting the men of Sodom with blindness (19:11), (2) they plainly said "THEY" were going to destroy Sodom and Gomorrah (19:13), (3) when the two said they (vs. 18 Lot addressed "them" as "Lord" vs.18, and "they" answered as "one".) would spare Zoar for Lot to retreat to (in19:21), also is a very strong proof that they were indeed the other two members of the Trinity, not recognized by Lot at first at the city gate.

Our Lord Jesus Christ as the "Word" or "Logos" was certainly "sent" into the world to bring salvation to lost mankind! (This usage of the term "angel" is found in Revelation with the letters to the seven "angels" of the seven churches of Asia ... which scholars identify as the "seven pastors of those churches.) Also, Jesus said plainly... He was going to "send" a comforter (Jn.16:7), the Holy Spirit, to convict the world of sin righteousness and judgment. If this is a correct understanding of the record then that would show why the scriptures plainly state that (Gen.19:24) "Then the Lord rained upon Sodom and upon Gomorrah brimstone and fire from the Lord out of heaven." (An interesting note here is that Lot addressed the 2 angels as one, "And lot said unto them, 'Oh not so my Lord' ... 19:18, as the scriptures in Gen.18 teach the same precedent, i.e. equality of the Godhead in speaking. Here, three were recognized as one as they were addressed as one /and as well they spoke as one.

Note also a further indication that these two were the "Lord" in vs.16, "..the men laid hold on his hand ...etc."the Lord being merciful unto him.." vs.17... "... that he said [singular two speaking as one as in Gen.18 where 3 spoke as one] escape for thy life".."lest thou be consumed ..." ... and Lot said unto them "Oh not so my Lord."vs.18 [singular for the two showing the Deity!] ... then vs.21."and he [the Lord/2 men] said unto him, see I have accepted thee concerning this thing, I will not overthrow this city..vs. 22" ....

I cannot do anything until thou come hither ... This is nicely capped off with vs.24.... "Then the Lord [the two sent members of the Trinity who led Lot and his family out of Sodom] rained upon Sodom and upon Gomorrah brimstone and fire from the Lord [the one who stayed behind with Abraham] out of heaven.)

It could therefore easily be translated or paraphrased as follows..." Then the two members of the trinity (the "Lord", yes the two also called "Lord", who went on ahead after communing with Abraham) who entered Sodom and removed Lot and his family, called down fire and brimstone from the "Lord" out of heaven (the other member of the Godhead who stayed behind and then left Abraham to depart directly back to heaven!). Amos 4:10-11 is even more plain, and irrefutably shows this paraphrase is indeed correct as follows, "...yet have ye not returned unto me saith the Lord (Jehovah) I have overthrown some of you as God (Jehovah) overthrew Sodom and Gomorrah, and ye were as a firebrand plucked out of the burning, yet have ye not returned unto me, saith the Lord." Remember the Psalmist plainly said that...." Thy throne O God is forever and ever the scepter of thy kingdom is a right scepter. Thou lovest righteousness, and hatest wickedness, <u>therefore God, Thy God</u> hath anointed thee with the oil of gladness above thy fellows ... Ps.45:6-7.

This is more clearly stated as quoted in Hebrews 1:8, "But unto the Son He saith Thy throne O God, is forever and ever: a scepter of righteousness is the scepter of thy kingdom." Plainly within the realm of scriptural soundness. This author has heard the shallow argument "well God is Omniscient/all knowing, and didn't have to visit Sodom to scope out it's wickedness." This argument certainly falls short when one considers that God did indeed <u>"come down"</u> to visit Abraham and said that He was "*GOING DOWN TO SODOM*"! (Gen18:21) The Divine Record speaks for itself!

One final proof text, to show the two angels who come to Sodom and Gomorrah were no doubt 2 "sent" members of the Godhead is found in Gen16:11 and 13. Here Hagar was visited by the "Angel /messenger of the Lord" vs.11 "And the <u>angel of the Lord said unto her</u> Behold, thou art with child, and shalt bear a son and shalt call his name Ishmael; because the Lord hath heard thy affliction", and the reply from Hagar is very plain indeed, "... and she called the name of <u>the Lord that spake unto her, Thou God</u> seest me: for she said Have I also here looked after him that seeth me?" The angel of the Lord was indeed a member of the Triune Godhead.

The "Lord Jehovah" appears as "Three Men"
(manifesting His triune 3 person in one Godhead)
and "His/Their" conservations with Abraham
and Lot broken down as follows:

Remember, God had already appeared to Abraham a number of times from Genesis chap. 12-ch. 17 personally and in a vision so Abraham was well acquainted with the Triune Godhead. Genesis 18:1 "... The Lord (Jehovah 3068) <u>appeared unto him</u> ..." Abraham saw three men, vs. 2 and the account is as follows:

Genesis 18:1. And the <u>Lord</u> (singular) appeared unto him in the plains of Mamre as he sat in the tent door in the heat of the day. And he lift up his eyes and looked and lo, <u>three</u> (plural) men stood by him: and when he saw them (plural) he ran to meet <u>them</u> (plural) from the tent door and bowed himself toward the ground. And said, "My <u>Lord</u> (singular to the three) if now I have found favor in <u>thy</u> (singular to the three) sight, pass not away I pray <u>thee</u> (singular to the three) from thy servant: Let a little water, I pray <u>you</u>, be fetched and wash your (plural pronoun) feet and rest <u>yourselves</u> (plural pronoun) under the tree and I will fetch a morsel of bread and comfort <u>ye your</u> (singular pronoun) <u>hearts</u> (plural); after that <u>you</u> (singular to the three) shall pass on for therefore are <u>you</u> (singular to the three) come to <u>your</u> (singular to the three) servant." And <u>they</u> (plural pronoun of the three) said, "So do as you have said."

Verse 8. "… and he stood by them (plural pronoun) under the tree and they (plural pronoun to the three) did eat. And they (plural pronoun) said unto him, "Where is Sarah your wife?" And he said, "Behold in the tent." And He (the Lord singular) said, "I (singular pronoun) will certainly return unto you according to the time of life, and lo Sarah your wife shall have a son …" Vs. 13, … and the Lord (singular pronoun) said unto Abraham … "did Sarah laugh saying shall I of a surety bear a child which am old?" Verse 14, The Lord (singular pronoun) speaking, "Is anything too hard for the Lord (singular pronoun) … at the time appointed I (singular pronoun) will return unto you according to the time of life … and He (the Lord singular pronoun) said, "… Nay but you did laugh." Verse 17 … and the Lord (singular pronoun) said, "Shall I hide from Abraham the thing which I (singular pronoun) do?"…

The simple fact here is that Abraham addressed the three as one and they answered and conversed as one entity between themselves and him. "Three in one, or one in three!

THE DIALOGUE WITH LOT AS FOLLOWS...

Genesis 19 "... and there came 2 angels to Sodom..."... ("Malaks" 4397 <u>Messengers</u> ... but messengers clearly identified as "God" whenever the Angel of God appeared in the Jewish Old Testament ... see comments in this booklet on "Angel of the Lord" under "Other Viewpoints" for further clarity ...

Chapter 19. In the previous chapter the Lord said "I will go down to Sodom ..." and He did so in the plurality of the other two members of the Godhead who went as 'messengers' for the other member who stayed behind talking with Abraham! At first Lot did not recognize them as being the 'Lord' and addressed them as 'lords,' verse 2. (Unfortunately the translators used the term 'angels' for the two who went down to Sodom.) Then they began speaking in unison again, verse 2, "... And they (plural/unison) said, "nay, but we will abide in the street ..." Verse 12, And the men said (again in unison) unto Lot "... hast thou any here besides." Notice vs. 13, "... we will destroy this place ...the Lord hath sent us to destroy it," and compare this to verse 24 which says, "... then the Lord (plainly the two members of the Godhead visiting Lot) rained upon Sodom and Gomorrah brimstone and fire from the Lord (the one member who stayed behind with Abraham and then departed back to heaven) out of heaven ..." Verse 17, "... when they (the two of the Godhead) had brought them forth (Lot and family out of Sodom) "... that He (singular) said escape ..." the two speaking as one! Then in verse 18 Lot speaking to the two, said "...

25

oh not so my Lord (as singular). Lot clearly recognized them as a plurality in unity! Notice verses 19-21, Lot continues talking/addressing them as one, and they, the two of the Godhead continue speaking as one.

> Vs. 24, 25... The Lord (the 2 with Lot) rained upon Sodom & upon Gomorrah brimstone and fire from the Lord (the one who stayed behind with Abraham) out of heaven; And He overthrew those cities, and all the plain and all the inhabitants of the cities, and that which grew upon the ground ...

Plainly the two who came to visit lot in chapter 19, were two members of the Godhead and were the same Heavenly Host who came to Jacob in Genesis chapter 32!

Just as Lot met the (angels) messengers at the gate of the city, so these same heavenly messengers came to Jacob in Genesis 32:1-2. "And Jacob went on his way, and the angels (messengers) of God met him. And when Jacob saw them he said, "This is God's host," and he called the name of that place Mahanaim. It is the highest probability that Jacob (like Lot) did not recognize at first that these were members of the Godhead. Also, that these were indeed the same two of the group that met with Abraham and Lot is no doubt a fact. It is evident that these two angel/messengers were sent on a mission to minister to Jacob as they did to

Abraham and Lot. Remembering these two of "God's host" appeared as normal looking men which helped them blend in well with Jacob and all of his traveling companions, until the time of their "blessing Jacob." Indeed one of them did just that vs. 24-29 when He as the Lord God, wrestled all night with Jacob. Jacob received a painful wound, but at the same time received the well deserved well earned blessing of vs.28, "…thou hast power with God and with men and hast prevailed."

Of course someone will ask the question "Then where was the other visiting heavenly man/angel/messenger?" (I.e. Trinity member). Our answer is the same as before …"He was where he wanted to be!" When Jacob wrestled with the "Man" it is plain to see and easy to believe from his exclamation in vs.30 ("And Jacob called the name of the place Peniel for I have seen "God" face to face and my life is preserved"), that the man was indeed "God" or one member of the blessed Triune Godhead! One other very important point as follows: While the Holy Scriptures are silent about where these two "angel/messengers of God" were when Jacob prayed to the "God of his fathers" in vs. 9-11, both were probably present as two members of the Trinity while he spoke to them this prayer. The prayer of course was addressed to them. This interpretation is based on the previous established precedent, the conversation Lot had with the 2 angel/messengers in chap. 19, when he plainly addressed the two as one, and they answered him in the singular form as Almighty God. See ch.19.vs. 18-21 for this "plural singular discussion" To those who say the Holy Spirit never takes a human form ... need to remember a. It certainly is possible since He is also omnipotent. b He did indeed appear in Acts in the form of a dove, in the form of cloven tongues of fire, and as a rushing mighty wind etc.

Rx FOR THE DIE-HARD RUCKMAN TYPE 1611 ONLY CROWD WHO SAY, "THE ENGLISH WORD <u>ANGEL</u> IS CORRECT AND NEVER MEANS GOD OR A MEMBER OF THE TRINITY.

Unfortunately there is the school of thought concerning the K.J.V. that teaches the false doctrines of Dr. Peter S. Ruckman. Ruckmanism is a true blight on the modern evangelical movement, dividing good men, and splitting Bible believing fundamental churches.

While this author will not attempt to expose his false doctrines in this booklet, it is only fair to say that his basic premise is that the 1611 K.J.V of the Bible was so "superintended by God" in its translation that it is infallibly correct in all of its translation and needs no Hebrew or Greek clarification at all ever. Now if the reader of this paper is of that persuasion, then the following will present quite a problem, i.e. the problem that the Bible must contradict itself if Ruckman is correct. This authors conviction is plain that the Word of God, the Bible is the inspired Word of God, and that only in very limited occurrences does the translation need clarification from the original tongues it was written in. (Yes no doubt, this author would love to see the demise and eradication of Ruckmanism).

PROOF (RX) AS FOLLOWS

It has been clearly established in Gen.32 that Jacob wrestled with a man who was truly an anthropomorphic manifestation of God, or one member of the Blessed Trinity. It is clearly evident that this "man" was one of the 2 angels who came (see vs.1 ch.32) to temporarily dwell with Jacob, bringing him a blessing, and was one of the same two who came to Lot in Gen.19. As well he was referred to as Deity when Jacob made the statement in vs.30 that he had seen GOD face to face and had lived. Now for the final proof to show that indeed in the Hebrew scripture that Almighty God, Jehovah was in one of His personages called an "Angel," (in the K.J.V.) showing the underlying Hebrew term "messenger" is indeed correct. The word "Angel" does not necessarily mean "created angelic being," but indeed can be used of one member of the Trinity on a messenger/mission for the other one or two of the Godhead. !

Hosea ch.12:vs.2-4,

> "The Lord hath also a controversy with Judah and will punish Jacob according to his ways ... he took his brother by the heel in the womb and by his strength he had power with God. YEA HE PREVAILED OVER THE ANGEL AND PREVAILED, HE WEPT AND

MADE SUPPLICATION TO HIM; HE FOUND
HIM IN BETHEL AND THERE HE SPAKE WITH
US, EVEN THE LORD OF HOSTS

Now the incontrovertible/irrefutable fact should forever
stand that the word "angel" as was translated in the English,
etc. does NOT necessarily mean "a created angelic being such
as a seraphim etc" but CAN REFER TO GOD OR ONE OR
TWO MEMBERS OF THE TRIUNE GOD HEAD ON A
MISSION FOR THE OTHERS! CASE CLOSED!

OTHER TRINITY MANIFESTATIONS

Two or three members of the Blessed Trinity appeared together
at one time is clearly revealed in Gen.18-19 & Ch.32:1. The
Lord did appear at times as "1-2-3" men, (with His magnificent
glory shrouded by a fleshly-human disguises) in human form
or He did not. It is evident that these three men of Gen.18:1.
Were of no difference in their appearance than common men.
2. They ALL had supernatural powers. 3. In Gen.18 and 19
they were constantly being referred to in "The Plural" yet when
they spoke they "Spoke as One."

They "Spoke as the Lord Jehovah speaking" (again 18:3-
10 compared to 19:16-25 which shows this magnificent revelation!). These are incontrovertible-irrefutable facts that cannot
be disputed! Why should the Church that our Savior founded

find fault and resist such self evident conclusions is beyond this authors comprehension! These wonderful proofs found in Gen.18&19 & Gen.32 (etc.), has the potential, in the hands of an evangelistic church, to overthrow "anti-Trinitarian" sentiments in the false cults of this world ... Mormons, Watchtower, and as well bring the Jewish/Muslim communities to proof that their theological outlook on the "Oneness" of God ... is indeed flawed and in need of major overhauling.

The Word of God must be understood as it is written ... and not as "people read into it their own ideas and false premises! May many souls be saved from these wonderful truths are indeed our prayer.[1]

---

1   The Lord, (the first Triune member who stayed behind w/Abraham) hath sent us to destroy it. For the Lord (vs. 14) will destroy this city. Notice here – The "us to destroy it" is said to show factual identity of the two as "Lord" since they said in vs. 14 that "The Lord will destroy this city and again as well "THEY" would destroy the city making them equal in essence and power to Almighty God, yes they were God...two members of the Trinity.

Chapter 18 –
The Trinity Visits Abraham

In researching information for this paper to date, this writer is not aware of any other authors, pastors, writers, commentators, Biblical expositors, et.al., in *church history* who have identified the three visitors to Abraham as the blessed triune God manifesting Himself in the form of 3 men. If this is the case you may ask, "How can you, the writer, come to such a conclusion?" The answer is simple. Genesis, Chapter Eighteen speaks for itself. When reading this account, the reader must accept what he reads as a true account of Jehovah appearing to Abraham, then believing this is the Trinity will be the only logical conclusion he could come to. Let us begin with Genesis 18:1: "And the LORD appeared unto him in the plains of Mamre: as he sat in the tent door in the heat of the day;" The word LORD is the Hebrews' (Jewish) name for God – JEHOVAH (Strong's 3068).

He is the Almighty God of the Universe. This Jehovah moved from the invisible state to the visible, or an anthropomorphic manifestation in human form.

The reader needs to take a careful look, and notice, when Jehovah manifested Himself, what did Abraham see? "And he lift up his eyes and looked, and, lo, **three men** stood by him: and when he saw *them*, he ran to meet them from the tent door, and bowed himself toward the ground," Problems with the passage occur when authors, such as Ryrie (in the "Ryrie Study Bible"), etc, say that only one was Jehovah and the other two were angels. Reader, was Ryrie inspired of God to make such a statement?

Certainly not! To say such a thing, and attempt to teach it as truth is to attempt to add to the WORDS OF GOD. Genesis 18 says nothing of two "created type angelic beings" accompanying Jehovah. (We need to stay with the inspired record, vs.2).

When Abraham saw the three (3) men he ran to them, bowed himself toward the ground, and addressed THEM as "My Lord". The term or title "Lord", here in the Hebrew, is Adonai (Strong's 136) which was used only of The Lord God of Heaven by the Hebrew. Adonai is never used as an indication of such as a lord of a province, or an earthly/human lord or master of people. From Strong's (1376) the word Gebiyr is used for a ruling lord or master. When Sara calls Abraham "lord" it is the term gebiyr, or (113) adon. Adon is sovereign, lord, master, owner, but is rarely if ever used for God. The divine record has already established that Jehovah is a plurality – more than one in unity (Gen. 1:1; 1:26; 11:7).

Especially important is Genesis 11:7. Here God says, "Let us go down and there confound their language". Just who do you suppose went down to Babel? I am asking you, "Who went down to Babel?" One member of the triune God? Was God confused in saying "Let us go down?" Did He not mean what He said or say what He meant?

The simple fact is that in Genesis 11:7 The Lord God Jehovah moved from (i.e., traveled from) heaven to earth in His plural Unity or with other members of His plurality (as He did later in Genesis 18). If one can accept this fact plainly spoken in God's Word then why would someone scoff at the manifestation of Adonai in His plurality in Genesis 18? This chapter in the Word of God, so plain, so explicit, is able to devastate all modern anti-Trinitarians sentiment (i.e., Watchtower, Mormons, modern Judaism), which have fallen into anti-Trinitarianism. The simple truth easily established in 11:7 is that when Jehovah comes to earth, on a very important mission, <u>He comes in His plural unity!</u> This point is soundly established. It cannot be negated by the modern consensus of popular theological speculation. I find it interesting that Ryrie, in his concordance reference Bible, could admit to one of the three men as being Jehovah, appearing in a physical body as a man, but dismisses the possibility of the other two members of the Trinity as having the same option (making them only created angels visiting Abraham <u>with</u> Jehovah.)

When Abraham addressed the three men, he knew that these were not simply three men in the ordinary sense of the word. He knew they were God manifested in human form. Again, he called them Adonai. Abraham spoke to these three men as both *singular* and *plural*, which would be in complete accord with the plurality-in-unity of the Triune God: Genesis 18:3-5 And said, "*My Lord*, (singular) if now I have found favor in thy sight, pass not away, I pray thee, from thy servant: Let a little water, I pray *you*, (singular) be fetched, and wash *your* (plural) feet, and rest *yourselves* (plural) under the tree: 5 And I will fetch a morsel of bread, and comfort *ye* (singular) *your* (plural) *hearts*; (plural) after that ye shall pass on: for therefore are *ye* (singular) come to *your* (plural) servant. And *they* (plural) said, so do, as thou hast said."

The above argument may well have some weakness as some of the dialogue could be used in very casual conversation. That weakness turns to strength in the light of the next argument. Genesis 18:5.... And they said, "So do, as thou hast said." This is the first time they speak in unison or as one in Chapter Eighteen. The point is this, no doubt, indicates the unity in thought of the triune God who is a plurality-in-unity. Read it again: "AND THEY SAID" This point strengthens the argument that Abraham knew exactly to whom he was talking. He was addressing the 3 as 1 or 1 as three in a complete unity as one. One brick cannot build a house, but ... stone upon stone, line upon line, precept upon precept ... (Isa. 28:10) ... the house will be built.[1]

The next verse concerning the three men speaking in unison to Abraham is verse 9-10: ***And they said unto him,*** "Where *is* Sarah thy wife?" And he said, Behold, in the tent. 10 ***And he said,*** (Jehovah again speaking) "I will certainly return unto thee according to the time of life; and, lo, Sarah thy wife shall have a son, and Sarah heard *it* in the tent door, which *was* behind him."

Once more, the three men are speaking in unison or speaking with one voice to Abraham. The Holy Spirit confirms in verse 10 that it was God doing the talking. They all spoke as one, and as

---

1   Many Christians proclaim that "God being omniscient already knew the conditions of Sodom & Gomorrah" and so thus inferring that he didn't need to go on to Sodom but sent the two angels. This creates scriptural contradictions if they were correct that God thus failed to fulfill his spoken word to personally go to Sodom to investigate as Gen. 18:20,21 plainly states. The fact is God/Jehovah did personally go to Sodom!

well they said "I": (singular) "will certainly return". It is interesting to note just how little that the Lord spoke in Chapter Eighteen. First, in verse five, "so do as thou hast said", and secondly, in verses 9-15 the Lord's declaration about Sarah, and then thirdly, the fairly long discourse with Abraham about the destruction of Sodom and Gomorrah. I am sure the Lord was deeply grieved over His journey to Sodom and Gomorrah. No doubt He was troubled indeed!

> To those who may say "unison speech or speaking as one" by the 3 members of the Trinity is too strange or far out to be considered, I would say the following. 1. Who has ever met/conversed with 3 members of the Trinity in person besides Abraham except Lot who conversed with 2 members of the Trinity as we have just seen in comments on Chapter 19. Who could tell us how and in what manner the 3 communicate (or communicated) with Abraham? 2. If the 3 were indeed the Triune Godhead then are they not in perfect harmony/agreement and in perfect accord with each other? If so, then why could they not speak all together as one? Is that impossible with God? 3. The divine record plainly used the (plural) term when it says, "… and they said unto him." The scriptures here do not "demand" a figurative interpretation of this account!! To say this account is figurative is to open the door into any wild interpretation desired!! Either the scripture means what it says or it does not.

The Scriptures are plain that the first two times the Lord spoke, the men (the Trinity incarnate) spoke in unison or spoke as one. This sets the precedent for the three men speaking in unison or as one in the third and last discourses. NOTE: NO OTHER PRECEDENT WAS SET, NOT ONE! Also, when the men "rose up" to leave, He (the Lord) couldn't be distinguished from "three men": three men in three separate bodies. What better disguise for the Lord of Glory (The Triune Godhead) than to appear as three normal men as He was about to enter Sodom and Gomorrah.

The argument for the three men being the Trinity is further confirmed in verses 17-19: "And the LORD said, Shall I hide from Abraham that thing which I do; 18: Seeing that Abraham shall surely become a great and mighty nation, and all the nations of the earth shall be blessed in him? 19: For I know him, that he will command his children and his household after him, and they shall keep the way of the LORD, to do justice and judgment; that the LORD may bring upon Abraham that which he hath spoken of him." This is the amazing account of the Lord conferring with Him-selves (the three men-God incarnate) about whether or not He should reveal the reason for His trip to Sodom. Notice there is no fourth person here, but rather the three conferring between themselves in perfect unity, and in one accord.

Would someone dare say that the Triune God was incapable of manifesting Himself as three men as many commentators, obviously do.

When Jacob wrestled with the stranger at night, just what

was his declaration? (Gen. 32:30) "And Jacob called the name of the place Peniel: for I have seen God face to face, and my life is preserved." No doubt someone is asking, "If this is the case with Jacob, then where were the other two members of the Trinity?" The answer to that is simple: first, the Scriptures do not tell us; second, no doubt they still existed; and thirdly, they were where they wanted to be! Finally, back to Genesis 18:33;

The one member of the Trinity who lingered behind to discuss/debate the fate of Sodom and Gomorrah with Abraham, afterwards, ascended back to heaven while the other two members of the Godhead went on ahead to Sodom. Here again, the simple truth of three separate and distinct persons which make up the Triune Godhead manifested as three separate men – The Triune God, disguised/encased/shrouded in human flesh, since no human can look directly upon God and live! Who now, can deny, that this is a wonderful, prophetical indication of the Lord's future intention of "Becoming Flesh" and dwelling among man as the Lord Jesus Christ!

SUMMARY:

Abraham called the three men (remember not 2 angelic created beings and 1 man) <u>Adonai</u>. We have already established Adonai is a Hebrew title for God and God only, which leads to the following self evident conclusions:

1. Abraham knew that though three visitors appeared, looking exactly like men in every sense, they were how-

ever, in reality, to be addressed as Deity for he called them <u>Adonai. </u>Abraham was not an idolater. To call anything, or anyone, less than God 'Adonai' would be blasphemous. Again, Adonai is used, in the Hebrew Scriptures, only of Jehovah God.

2. The fact that the three men answered Abraham in unison or in one voice together, proves he was not speaking to just one of the men, but to all three. Had two of them been lesser than God, "<u>then for them to have</u> <u>answered as one in unison with God</u>" would have meant they received a "<u>false recognition of being equal to Jehovah</u>". If that would have been the case I am sure Jehovah's trip would have been cut short, and there would have been two more fallen angels. Remember, angels only have to sin once to be lost.

3. These three men were NOT distinguishable from each other. No indication in the Scriptures for that at all.

"JEHOVAH AND THREE ANGELS OR MEN APPEAR"

This "anti-Trinitarian argument is often used to attempt to discredit the possibility of Divine incarnation or condescension of Deity into human flesh. Satan hates that simple truth, and viciously attacks it in Gen.18-19 so that the incarnation of the "Word" becoming flesh, i.e. Jesus Christ as Deity come in the flesh, would become a mental/theological absurdity. Many Christians have readily accepted the false premise that "Jehovah did indeed come to Abraham, but *with* three men. The way this is presented, is where it says, Gen.18:1, "And the Lord appeared to him"...this is where Jehovah only supposedly appears (1), and then where it says vs.2, "And he lift up his eyes and looked and lo three men stood by him"... (and this is where the three men are supposed to appear (2). At first glance it seems to be a plausible rendering of the account, but the following must be considered!

Looking forward to Lot and the two "angels" who visited him it is clearly seen that TWO and ONLY TWO visited him, and when he was carrying on conservation with the TWO of them, vs.19-22, that the conversation as recorded in the Hebrew/Jewish Word of God goes to the SINGULAR ADDRESSING OF ONE DIVINE PERSON! Notice vs.18, "And Lot said unto them, Oh not so my Lord...grace in your sight ... and you have magnified ... vs.21 And HE said unto Lot ... See I have accepted you ... I will not overthrow ... I cannot do vs.22 ... vs.24 ... And the LORD (the two members of the Godhead speaking with Lot) ... rained upon Sodom and upon Gomorrah fire and brimstone from the LORD (the other member of the Godhead who stayed behind with Abraham and went straight back to heaven) out of heaven. Plain indeed that the Lord Jehovah was talking to Lot in the form of "two men" and not two angels and Jehovah separately! Now in reflecting this back to Abraham and the 3 men visiting him, it is plain to see, since there were not "three with Lot" then there were not four meeting with Abraham when the Lord was plainly speaking to him! Another note of special consideration is that when Abraham was talking to Jehovah, Jehovah was in a "VISIBLE FORM" vs.1, so when the Lord said he was going down to Sodom, then it is a self evident fact that He must have been VISIBLE to Lot also in the dialogue of vs.18-22! This then further validates that since there were only two men/angel/messengers with Lot then "THEY were the "VISIBLE" Adonai/Lord speaking to Lot, i.e. two members of the blessed Trinity! A further proof that Jehovah did not appear WITH three men is the fact as follows: If there were three men with Jehovah, then when Abraham saw them off in vs.16 (still engaging the Lord in conservation in verses 23 on) then what happened to the "third" man when the angel/messengers reached Sodom since only 2 arrived there in 19:1?

The simple fact is that the Lord remaining talking to Abraham was indeed one of the three "men" putting to death the false idea of the Lord and 3 men appearing to Abraham.... Simple when vs.1 says that ..."And the Lord appeared to Abraham ... he lifted up his eyes and saw THREE MEN" that there were THREE and only THREE beings present and they were indeed "God manifested in the flesh to Abraham". Lastly ... to those who would use Lot's utterance of "Adon"113 or master to the two men, yes is a fact of Holy Writ, but is only an indication that Lot was erring on the side of caution since no doubt his spiritual maturity nowhere matched that of Abraham. Abraham freely used the term "Adonai" 136, to the three men, while

Lot no doubt never had personally come into contact and conversation with the Deity and did not want to ascribe Deity to 2 beings that appeared to be two men travelers. At first meeting with them at the gate of the city, he was had no idea the men were really two of the Godhead. .

The Key to Unlock

To unlock the Truth that Genesis 18 certainly does reveal a Triune Godhead appearing to Abraham in anthropomorphic form is found clearly (yet somewhat subtly) in the following key:

THE KEY

Three places in Genesis (a). The three men were addressed as Adonai. (b). They, the three, spoke and addressed Abraham as "one" which demands recognition for the three as <u>Deity speaking</u> and not only as "one" of the three speaking to him. Even if one of the three were speaking for all three, then that would give the other two recognition of Deity also. Considering all this, Theodore Patai's confusion (next page following) is put to rest.

TO RECAP THIS KEY

1. When God appeared to Abraham - Abraham bowed down before them & addresses them as Adonai, Genesis 18:1-3.

2. "They" (vs.9) asked Abraham where his wife was and then "they" said "I" will return to you... (vs. 10). Here if "they" were two angels and Jehovah, then two angels were given recognition as "God" when the "I will return" was spoken! Thus the three men were indeed God veiled in human flesh.

3. (vs. 33) states " And the Lord went his way as he left over communing with Abraham...shows (a) the three men (God) departed from Abraham, (b) to perform their (HIS) intended (personal) visit to Sodom as He/God promised (vs. 20,21). So...one of the God head returned to heaven from Abraham, while the other two traveled to Sodom as messengers (angels in the English) for the other (the one who returned to heaven).

This author is firmly convinced God intended for Genesis 18 to reveal His Triune being. To use the weak argument "The Holy Spirit and/or The Father would not take human form, but the LOGOS "WORD" only would, forget that each member of the Trinity is coequal, coexistent, coeternal with the others and nothing is outside the realm of God's possibility or powers. Christians today easily proclaim the wonderful truth that indeed our bodies are the Temple of the Holy Spirit, the third member of the Godhead.

Genesis 18 & 19

Part V:
Viewpoints from Theodore Patai

Upon nearing the completion of this booklet, my good friend and co-laborer in soul winning in the prisons, Dr. Kenneth Lierle (Director of Bethesda Mission School.) brought to my attention a strictly secular non-Christian source, which clearly proved the following:

1.   That Judaism in O.T. Bible times historically held a pluralistic view of God, i.e. more than one person in the God Head.

2.   That Genesis 18 was indeed a proof of that point.

This source claimed a seeming contradictory mystery where 2 of the 3 in one deity of Chapter 18 "changed over" into two angels by the time they reached Sodom in Chapter 19 (See our notes on chapter 19 proof that the 2 messengers/angels were indeed the two other members of the Trinity).

The fact that this source is indeed strictly secular and non-Christian, is stunning and absolutely amazing. The church under the teaching of misled commentators has obscured, over looked, and yea, even degraded the literal understanding of Gen 18 & 19. This non-Christian source has correctly identified it at least in secular eyes "the truth of the triune Godhead, one God in three persons in Genesis 18!"

Amazing Non Christian Recognition of The Trinity In Genesis Chapter 18 as Follows…

Theodore Patai (Wayne State University Press, Detroit) anthropologist and writer concerning middle Eastern Jewish cultures correctly reads and understands Genesis 16. Naturally Patai stumbles at Genesis 19 by failing to understand the two angels of Chapter 19 were indeed two of the same company of the three of Genesis 18. Before this author quotes Patai one more note needs to be made concerning the seeming 'split' of two of the three men from the group meeting with Abraham as they were departing from their visit. The seeming 'split' explained in verse 22, "… and the men turned their faces from thence and went towards Sodom, but Abraham stood yet before the Lord. Vs. 23, "… and Abraham drew near and said, "… wilt thou also destroy the righteous with the wicked?" The answer as follows:

First…. remember that there were three men that were addressed as "Adonai" in Gen 18 which shows that the 2 departing in verse 22 were equally God.

Secondly…. these 2 men (these two of the Trinity) in 18:22 turned their faces towards Sodom.

Thirdly…. the divine record states "… but Abraham stood yet before the Lord…I.e.-He stood in front of and face to face

**with the Lord or one of the Triune Godhead (or Adonai) whom
he was respectfully confronting.** Abraham was confronting the
Lord pleading with him for the sparing of the cities for the righteous' sake. Remember again the three men were already addressed
as Adonai in 18:3, so any one of them was equally "the Lord".

Fourthly....(a) the Triune God Head/Adonai manifested as
three men faced Abraham & Sarah together in their appearance (Gen 18:1); (b) consulted together between themselves
about destroying Sodom & Gomorrah (vs. 17-19); (c) they discussed together with Abraham their intent to go down and see
firsthand the conditions of Sodom & Gomorrah (vs.20,21); (d)
thus they (two of the Godhead) headed toward Sodom (vs.22-
23), and they arrived there to be met by Lot at the gates of the
city in Chapter 19! The mission of the Lord God was to go to
Sodom, and had to be fulfilled for the Lord Adonai to keep His
word. The word of God had to be fulfilled!

This author, a writer of fundamental biblical apologetical
literature, finds it quite an anomaly to be referencing the works
of a strictly secular source who unwittingly exonerates the
teaching of the Trinity/Triune Godhead as revealed in Gen 18-
19. Why have the evangelical fundamentalist churches and its
favorite commentaries &. commentators so ignored, and even
dogmatically overlooked the correct understanding of Gen 18
& 19? That does remain a mystery that this author cannot explain with Patai. It would certainly seem , maybe, that the Lord
has opened the mouth of Balaam's mule to shame the prophet
(the churches in this case)!

Quotations from the book as follows from "The Hebrew Goddess," Rapheal Patai, Wayne State University Press, Detroit, as follows.. pgs 110 & 111 (under conclusion). *"In Biblical times there was nothing strange, let alone heretical, about a plural concept of the Godhead. Most of the Nations in whose midst Israel dwelt recognized divine pluralities, and the old Hebrew myth (Patai speaking) saw nothing remarkable in the fact that Yahweh appeared to Abraham in the shape of three men who, however, were unhesitatingly recognized by Abraham as ONE PERSON. The narrative is masterly in conveying the mystery of these three in one deity by <u>changing back and forth between plural and singular, to which has to be added the further mystery of the unexplained change over of the three men into two angels by the time they reached Sodom and their contradictory identification as Yahweh's messenger."</u>* (end of quote).

Here Patai has, the honesty and integrity to read and take literally what is said in Genesis 18. Though he may not consider it to be the inspired word of God is irrelevant. The fact is there are many secular anthropological/historians who regard both the Old & New Testament to be accurate historically while not necessarily considering the record to be given by inspiration of God!

PATAI'S HONEST CONCLUSION

(#1)...Notice how well Patai fronts the historical conclusion that there was nothing strange about the Hebrews in Biblical times embracing a plural concept of the Godhead! Perhaps that may well explain why the Israelites in Old Testament times were so susceptible to straying at times they accepted false gods or goddesses, such as the gods of Egypt such as Isis Osiras or perhaps even Semarimas as part of their belief in a plural Godhead! The fact also stands out that with a true Biblical original view of a plural Godhead, united as one, could well explain the temptation to see God as not only masculine but feminine in a plural concept. Rafael Patai, reflecting God's creation of man & woman, i.e...."two shall be one flesh" since man was created in the image of God points out that the Shekinah was looked upon by some Hebrews, whom had drifted into apostasy, as being the feminine member of the Godhead. Modern day Judaism has certainly not been taught this historical fact.

Had it been the modem day Jewish person could much more easily be won to Christ. (There are some groups of Jewish women who, since women's lib, have formed prayer and study groups to revive this ancient belief). Certainly it would be much easier to show that one member of the Godhead condescended to incarnate himself in human flesh through the womb of the virgin Mary, to be born as the Divine Son of God/Jewish Messiah. Isaiah 7:14 tells us "Therefore the Lord himself shall give you a sign behold a virgin shall conceive and bare a son and shall call his name "Immanuel", and also Isaiah 9:6 which says for unto us a child is born, unto us a son is given and the government shall be upon his shoulder and his name shall be called Wonderful, Counselor, The Mighty God, The Everlasting Father and The Prince of Peace". (Thus the incarnate one the "WORD", being himself equal with God.)

(#2)... Notice Patai so clearly understands as the Mosaic record says that Yaweh (sic) ... appeared to Abraham in the form of 3 men ..." Now here is where modern commentaries have egregiously desecrated, yea and have even (yes ignorantly) blasphemed a major cornerstone of the Judeo Christian Faith. How dare any person especially one who accepts the divinely inspired word of God, pervert the plain fact of "three men appearing" into "Jehovah and two angels appearing"!? This fact "three men", coupled with his next point (which endorses this authors previously drawn conclusion) proves three men were indeed the Triune Godhead in physical revelation!

Patai says three"... Of three men who, were unhesitatingly recognized by Abraham as one person the narrative is masterly in conveying the mystery of this three in one deity by changing back and forth between plural and singular ..." I could not have stated this fact concerning the conversation between Abraham and the three men anymore persuasively than Patai who does not even claim to be a born again Christian!

Years ago when this author would read this narrative (and conversation) while holding the false idea of Jehovah and two angels being involved in a discussion with Abraham, I could not understand the shift from plural to singular, back and forth. At first I thought that perhaps there was a secret "super imposing" of two different narratives or stories in the chapter. I divided the story into two separate accounts on paper writing down two stories, (one with the singular, and one with the plural), hoping to make sense of it. Example is verses 9&10, where verse 9 says "then said they unto Abraham, Where is Sarah your wife?" So Abraham said, "here in the tent", (vs. 10) and He said ... " I will certainly return to you according to the time of life and behold, Sarah your wife shall have a son". Also note verse 3: Abraham addressed the three men as "... My Lord...." Then in verse 4 "... Rest yourselves and then verse 5 "... they said (shows they spoke in unison) do as you have said." Saying that here one of them was Jehovah and one was speaking as a representative for Jehovah for all 3 simply is not supported by the text. That is without dispute.

Naturally, If one thinks this narrative needs to be interpreted then such could be the case, but this would cause the possibility to say this entire chapter is merely a parable and not literally true. This in turn would open the door to literally any interpretation no matter how far out! Sorry, the record speaks for itself and can not be understood to teach anything but that God is a Triune, Divine being i.e. three persons in One !!

Honesty is the sole means of understanding chapter 18 & 19. The phrase (18:33) "... the Lord went his way ..." (here again the two departing and being referred to as one ... i.e. "Lord") plainly shows that the one member of the Godhead who stayed behind, (to negotiate with Abraham), left to ascend back to heaven while the other 2 (members of the Godhead) went on ahead. To presume 2 men, (members of the Godhead) going on ahead totally without the third to investigate Sodom & Gomorrah is not to violate the truth of Gen 18 since the two were equally the Lord! To say this author is making much to do about nothing is to:

1. Endorse the dishonoring of the revelation of God who plainly revealed himself to mankind as one God in three persons.

2. Uphold the perversion of divine record by misled commentators and their false erroneous footnotes on Genesis 18 & 19 (Scofield is not strangely silent on Genesis 18 since he lacked theological/moral credibility. See footnotes on Scofield below.)

3. Encourage anti-Trinitarianism to flourish.

How easy is it to see the New Testament truth established in 1 Timothy 3:16: Without controversy great is the mystery of Godliness, God was manifest in the flesh ..." and also John 1:1 "In the beginning was the Word and the Word was with God and the word was God" ... and verse 14" ... and the word was made flesh and dwelt among us..." Simply stated one member of the Godhead condescended to human form to become literally "God in the flesh" and as the embryo was conceived in the womb of the virgin Mary by one personage of the Godhead, The Holy Spirit and then the "Logos" (WORD) entering and taking possession of it, thus the embryo became the "Son of God" or literally "God in the flesh". It is my prayer that this booklet will exonerate the wonderful truth of the Triune Godhead revealed in Genesis 18.[1]

---

1 An interesting note on C. I. Scofield. If Rev. Scofield were alive to day his theological/moral foundation from his purported conversion to evangelical Christianity in 1879 on, would be soundly rejected by the present theological / pastoral community! 1 Tim 3:2,4 states; "A bishop must be blameless, the husband of one wife, vigilant, sober, of good behavior, given to hospitality, apt to teach, one that ruleth well his own house, having his children in subjection with all gravity." His conversion in 1879 did not keep him from six months in jail on forgery charges. After entering his "New Christian Life" he became a lawyer (and politician) and was admitted to the bar with no formal training, became engaged in a number of financial scams and spent six months in jail for forgery. (See historist.com/atricles2/ schofield.htm) Scofield also (subsequent to his conversion) totally abandoned his Roman Catholic wife and two small daughters, moved to Canada for a a time, returned and in 1883 began dating 2 women while still married to his wife. (During this time he defrauded his mother in law out of $1300.00 with a forged mortgage which she was unable to collect When he had the means to repay the false investment he never did) This same year she divorced him for abandonment, (were today's laws on child support been in place then, he would no doubt have been put in jail for lack of child support 1 Tim 5:8 states; But if any provide not for his own, and especially for those of his own house, he has denied the faith and is worse than an infidel (unbeliever). He married one of the two women, Hettie Hall Von Wartz, and amazingly was ordained absolutely no college or university credits to its due. Amazingly, churches today who proudly refuse to admit a twice married, (divorced) Pastor/Minister to their pulpit or ordination committee, do admit honor and extol Scofield and his Bible to theirs. His supporters were (and still are) careful not to admit to his marital/educational/financial past. To say it matters not about his past is to say "Character matters not" about ones entrance into Christian Ministry. See also the website poweredbychrist.homestead.com/files/cyrus/schofield.htm

Part VI:
The Church vs. the
Trinity of the Old Testament

After closely examining (Gen. 18 &19) it is evident that the Christian church, as a whole, has failed to recognize the invaluable Trinitarian truths contained in these two chapters! The anti-trinitarians, and the anti-deity of Christ religious groups and sects, mostly accept the Old Testament as Divinely inspired books, but fail to recognize and acknowledge that Jesus Christ was indeed literally God come in the flesh. This clearly shows that the church of Christ or the body of Christ has failed to recognize the prophetical deity of Christ in Genesis 18 & 19 and has as well:

A. Failed to recognize the Trinity manifested in human form in Genesis 18&19, and thus allows anti-Trinitarians to flourish

B. Failed to accept as a fact of Holy Writ the blessed Trinity in Genesis 18 due to the influence of well meaning Biblical scholars who have refused to accept this chapter at face value, reading into it anti-Trinitarian concepts using Gen. 19 with the 2 angels (inferring the angel messengers as being two created beings) to reverse interpret Gen. 18! (Ryrie, Thompson Chain, and a host of others).

C. Failed to (by falsely interpreting Gen 18) have at its disposal the most powerful overlooked tool in its arsenal to overthrow anti-Trinitarian sentiments.

D. Failed to reach the Jewish Community with Trinitarian doctrine. The truth of Genesis 18 gives potential for bringing them to Christ as a nation and possibly produce the budding of the fig tree. This Old Testament doctrine could lead to the restoration of Israel as a nation to God, and recognition of Jesus Christ, her promised Messiah.

E. Failed to overthrow the false anti-Trinitarian views of Charles Taze Russell (Watchtower or self professed/ wrongly called Jehovah Witnesses), Joseph Smith (Mormans) and all other anti-Trinitarian false religionists who will perish without knowing the truth.

F. Failed to understand the responsibility to read and accept God's word at face value in opposition to shallow Biblical exegesis while bowing to isogenies by well meaning scholars. Recently I asked a Bible expositor, (an A.P. with over 60 years of service in Bible teaching who was and is well acquainted with this writers views on Genesis 18 & 19, but disagrees), just what reasons he could give me from these chapters, to disprove my argument. "No reasons," he said, "I just believe you are wrong." i.e. No scriptural basis for his unbelief.

NEBUCHADNEZZAR AND THE TRINITY

The trinity is not plainly taught in the O.T.? A plurality of more than one in the Godhead is not plainly taught? The antiquity of the book of Daniel easily goes back 500-600 years B.C. so it would be well to examine this book for clear Trinitarian/plurality of the Godhead teaching. This book plainly reveals that Daniel and King Nebuchadnezzar both believed in and taught the doctrine of the plurality of the Godhead, or one God in more than one person. Notice first ch.4 vs. 8 of the book of Daniel. Nebuchadnezzar readily acknowledged that the Spirit of the "**Holy Gods**" ("Gods in Hebrew also translated as "Saints" in Strongs 6918 and 6922 as "Qadosh) indwelt the prophet Daniel! "… and in whom is the spirit of the **Holy Gods** and before him I told the dream…."

Now Nebuchadnezzar certainly was no theologian, but his spiritual understanding at least was aware (no doubt by some minor theological education) that there was a plurality in the Godhead or the "Most High" that ruled the heavens! Now notice as follows….

1. Vs.9. … I know that the <u>Spirit</u> of the <u>Holy Gods</u> is in thee … (speaking to Belteshazzar concerning his dream).

2.   2. Vs.13. "… Nebuchadnezzar saw a "watcher and a <u>Holy One</u>", or one of the <u>Holy Ones</u> (one of the triune Most High) come down from the heavens.

3.   3. Vs.17. The judgment announced against himself was by "demand of the word of the <u>Holy Ones</u>" by decree of the watchers.

4.   4. He (Nebuchadnezzar) to Belteshazzar vs.18… about the interpretation of the dream … thou art able for the <u>Spirit of the Holy Gods</u> is in thee…."

Notice next when Daniel had the vision of the ram and the goat that there were two "Saints" or two "<u>Holy Ones</u>" (i.e. yes no doubt two members of the Trinity and no doubt the same "2" which appeared to Abraham/Lot and Jacob) standing next to him (Dan.8:13-14), with one directing the other to tell Daniel how long the period of time would be concerning the vision. The word translated "Saint" here is the same as "Holy" in the Hebrew, 6918 and 6922 or "Qadosh". No doubt here a visitation of the same "<u>Holy Ones</u>" which were referred to in ch.4. Isaiah 60:9&14 as follows…. "… the Lord thy God and the Holy one of Israel" … and vs.14 … "… the Zion of the Holy One of Israel." Notice also Isaiah 6:3 "… And one cried unto another and said, **Holy Holy Holy** is the Lord of hosts: the whole earth is full of His glory." Here the three personages of the Holy Trinity no doubt are referred to!

Here again clear indication that the Lord is a God of multiple personalities or three in one. To those who would use the very shallow argument that Nebuchadnezzar was a heathen king who worshipped many false gods, falls apart when it is realized that Daniel indeed interpreted the dream as a correct dream from the Most High which thus endorsed the "Spirit of the Holy Gods" mentioned in these chapters! A last note of interest here is that if the "Spirit" of the "Holy Gods" dwelt in Daniel ... then that would plainly mean there were at least two "Holy Gods" left in heaven! One plus two equals three ... the Triune God head ... the Holy One of Israel ... one God with 3 distinct personalities. One last thought here, Daniel 3:28-29 and 4:8&9 shows he did "**NOT**" worship false gods, but accepted the God of Daniel as his God also!

LOT EXONERATED

For years and years, every time this author has heard Lot's name mentioned by pastors in a sermon, he is made to be a backslider, carnal, compromiser who deserted Abraham and his God by "choosing the well watered plains of Jordan"(Gen. 13:10) and then "pitching his tent toward Sodom." This shallow exegesis on Lot by these pastors, etc, naturally makes him look very carnal/unspiritual from the beginning. However! It must be noted that Abraham would have done exactly the same thing Lot did,(pitched HIS tent toward Sodom) had Lot chosen the land of Canaan!

Did not Abraham say he would go whichever way Lot did not go? Vs.9 says such! So plainly there was no choice to "do evil" by Lot choosing Jordan! To say so is to contradict scripture and read into it that which it says not! To say Abraham, or God, was scheming/testing Lot by giving him a choice between good and evil is to say 1. Abraham helped stumble Lot towards a disastrous choice, 2. That Abraham didn't care Lot chose the evil path since he gave Lot the green light to proceed in that direction with no rebuke or warning. NO! This certainly could not have been the case! Righteous Abraham could have easily and willingly "pitched HIS tent toward Sodom" had righteous Lot chosen Canaan. Also note that Canaan was noted for the wicked and depraved Canaanites which dwelt there, so should we say Abraham "pitched his tents towards the wicked Canaanites" thus compromising the command to be "separate from evil"? This plainly exonerates Lot in his choice to choose Jordan! Next, we'll examine Lot and his family eventually journeying to/and beginning to dwell in Sodom, Gen. 13:12.

BUT FIRST

II Pet.2:7-8-9: "… And delivered _Just_ Lot, vexed with the filthy conversation of the wicked (for that <u>righteous man </u>dwelling among them, in seeing and hearing vexed his <u>righteous</u> <u>soul</u> from day to day with their unlawful deeds). The Lord knoweth how to deliver the _godly_ out of temptations and to reserve the unjust unto the day of judgment to be punished: …

Notice carefully here, 1. Lot was indeed vexed/disgusted/ etc. by seeing and hearing the wickedness of the ungodly Sodomites he was dwelling closely to. 2. The scripture is clear Lot was NOT involved with, nor partaking in the wickedness of Sodom and Gomorrah. How many of the readers of this booklet are "living in a city" ... or close to a city? So condemn Lot?

What city in 2019 is NOT involved in the same depravity and sinfulness that was evident in Sodom (as well as in the entire world)? How many millions of precious innocent babies are butchered every year in the abortion mills in the U.S.A? The air waves ... yea every square foot of air space has electronic filth and porn flowing through it like a sewer from hell through what is called electronic communication! What about sexual perversion/ homosexuality and lesbianism gaining such favor that marriage for them has been and is being endorsed in cities and states here and around the world? And yet preachers and Bible commentators have the nerve to single out Lot and infer he was a "backslidden wicked compromiser by living near to and in Sodom when they themselves are doing the same ... living in wicked U.S.A. cities.! Oh yes ... they must get a pass....

"They are doing God's bidding in the country by preaching and winning souls ... representing righteousness and building churches for the fields here are white unto harvest" ... but Lot ... Lot must be condemned for where he was ... (I seriously doubt that very few if any of the "preachers of righteousness" today would be willing to go back and stand in Lots' shoes as a testimony to the wicked in Sodom and Gomorrah!)

Oh no! ... He couldn't have been doing the Lord's bidding of holding the torch of righteousness in the gate of the wicked city of Sodom and Gomorrah preaching and testifying to those wicked people! The real truth must be, that the cities of S&G "owed" Abraham one, (and naturally thus Lot as well) for rescuing them and their goods from King Chedorlaomer which no doubt gave Lot enough favor with them that they reluctantly tolerated his preaching! (The main difference today is there are "many" righteous people living in the wicked Sodom and Gomorrah's of the world).Lot cannot be condemned! God thought enough of Lot to "PERSONALLY" escort him out of the city with his family ... LOT WAS HONORED BY GOD!

Would these ministers be honored by God in like manner should their wicked city be brought to incineration? Lot was called Righteous, Just, and Godly, as well he was targeted by the Lord to be removed from Sodom that the cities could be punished! These three verses in Peter are clear on that point. To condemn Lot for where he lived is to condemn all Christians no doubt, for where they live today, unless they live in a wilderness and away from everyone else, and are completely self supporting and home schooling their children! What Hypocrisy! Dare anyone single Lot out and point a finger at him! Yes this author is convinced that Lot was indeed "preaching righteousness" to those wicked of the cities ... doing the Lord's bidding before judgment fell! Does God send fire and brimstone upon a wicked people without warning them first? NEVER ... NEVER!

This precedent of "Divine warning preceding Divine judgment" is firmly established in Scripture and is very clear, so it must also be applied to S&G! Lot was the only righteous man there so his righteousness must have been declared through preaching to those ungodly sinners. I am amazed that today, pastors, Bible/seminary teachers and professors etc, will stand and pontificate against truly righteous Lot, attempting to dredge up something against him, when the Word of God says nothing against him at all! How many of Lot's critics are truly "soul winners" reaching the lost with the gospel? While pontificating against him, they themselves will refuse to be active in soul winning visitation programs, witnessing to their neighbors and friends, but yes they can stand in their pulpits and lecture stands to "proclaim the glories of God to the righteous." They will gladly scramble to preach and teach anywhere the righteous will sit in awe and admiration, but will cringe and cower to go to the prisons, hedges highways and byways to warn the wicked to repent! The "fruit of the Righteous is the tree of life and he that winneth souls is wise." Prov.11:30.

I never have known a truly righteous minister/or saint who was silent in his witness for Jehovah/Jesus. Certainly Lot could have chosen to go to the wilderness totally away from all of wicked civilization! Would he then be exonerated as being separate from evil?

How many pastors, missionaries fresh out of seminary/theological school, head to cities here in America and other countries of the world which are teeming with sin and corruption (of course taking along their children and wives) to start/and or pastor Bible believing churches?

Do they "head to the wilderness to be separated from the

sinners and evil of the Land? If these cities need a witness for the Lord then we can be certain Sodom and Gomorrah deserved at least to hear of Jehovah and His truth (as did Ninevah and Noah's generation) before the Lord burnt them with fire and brimstone! It is plainly stated in Gen.14:11 "And Abram said to the king of Sodom, I have lift up mine hand unto the Lord, the most high God, the possessor of heaven and earth." Abraham was exalting the truth of the only true and righteous God of heaven is self evident here. This proclamation was shortly before the cities were incinerated.

The scriptures teach that God has no pleasure in the death of the wicked! Lot cannot be condemned for his chosen place of farming/working /dwelling in light of the Lords desire to see men repent and be forewarned of coming judgment. It must be also remembered that the two kings, (Gen.14:2-4) of Sodom and Gomorrah, Bera and Birsha previously had tasted total defeat and humiliation under the hand of King Chedorlaomer as well were enslaved by him for 13 years! When the kings of S&G finally rebelled against him and fled to the slime pits of Sidim, Chedorlaomer ravished S&G, took all of its goods, and as well took Lot and his goods captive (14:11-12).

Upon hearing this information Abraham took his servants, pursued Chedorlaomer 1. Destroyed him and his armies, 2. Brought back S&G's goods, as well as Lot and his goods, 3. Delivered back to the Kings of S&G their goods and persons seized by Chedorlaomer. 4. Refused to keep the goods offered to him by the 2 kings (vs.21-24). It must be remembered that these cities were termed as "wicked and exceedingly sinful before the Lord" (13:13). Modern and as well skewed theological opinion probably would have encouraged Abraham to refuse to go rescue "backslidden perverted Lot", to allow him to suffer, as well they would probably have Abraham refuse to give back the "goods" to the kings of S&G so they would suffer and die due to their wickedness! I am wondering why they are silent and not condemning Abraham for rescuing "wicked backslidden Lot" and as well honoring the kings of S&G by returning their goods that they could continue to prosper?!

The truth is simple here. Lot was not a "wicked backslidden perverted man" but a "righteous, Godly, just man"....2Pet.2:7-9, and as well no doubt the Lord wanted to give S&G space and time to consider their wickedness to repent before judgment fell.(This author wonders how the "Calvinists" who falsely imagine that "God ordains all things, thoughts and actions", can explain why God ordained the two cities to be incinerated, and consigned to eternal hell fire after, in eternity past, designing their lack of repentance and eternal damnation! Calvinism is a damnable heresy! Imagine God supposedly, ordaining some to believe and be saved, and most others ordained to be eternally damned with no hope on their part of repentance! Heretic John Calvin plainly taught "double predestination ... that is a fact. The kings were, enslaved and tormented by their enemies for 13 years. Their cities were ravished/raped and degraded, and they fled to the slime pits, finally were rescued by Abraham a "man of God" and restored to their cities by him!

Then there is the finger pointing at Lot's "offering his virgin daughters" to those wicked men in place of the 2 "men" messengers. Consider the following facts, (1). Lot gave misleading information about his daughters (19:8) to those wicked men in Sodom claiming they were virgins, when in reality they were married vs.14. Here he was clearly "grasping at straws" to slow down/sidetrack an extremely volatile situation!

What minister or righteous man would admit to an armed home invading rapist, that he had 2 lovely daughters hiding in another room if asked if there were any one else in the house? (2). Misleading information in such cases is justified and intended to "protect" not to unrighteously degrade/destroy the innocent. (3). That he was a righteous, just, godly man proves he would NOT have actually "given" his daughters to the men. He was clearly "buying time" desperately trying to defuse this situation. (4). Lot was not rebuked for this ploy ... rather the Lord smote the wicked without the door with blindness and that certainly did defuse the attempted attack.(An interesting side note here: There has always been the mistaken idea that S&G were huge cities ... may be into the hundreds of thousands ... but the scripture here seems to indicate differently. Vs.4, ch.19 ... "... the men of Sodom ... both old and young, All the people from every quarter ..." This seems to indicate the number of persons surrounding the house probably were only into the hundreds and hundreds, not thousands of thousands! Probably small cities indeed ... thus indicating much smaller cities than imagined.) The fact the Lord came personally to Lot and his family to rescue them was certainly no rebuke to him being a wicked fallen hypocrite, but rather to his honor as being a truly righteous/godly man. No! Lot was not a wicked, perverted, compromising backslider as most critics would paint him to be.

Lastly ... we need to consider Lot's daughters and their "sexual escapade" with their father. For anyone to even insinuate, or infer, that these physical sexual contacts were some sort of "incestuous lustful sexual orgy" is to plainly pervert Holy Scripture. First ... Lot and his daughters left Zoar for the mountains to dwell in a cave ... no doubt Lot fearing the "wickedness of that city, and possibly coming judgment later on it ... and desiring to be separate from those wicked people ... remember the Lord <u>was</u> going to destroy Zoar as well ... but spared it for Lot's sake ... 19:21) Now the daughters were basically clueless as to the future ... No men in the mountains ... No return to Zoar (women of that era did not take it upon themselves to be independent of their fathers (as it should still be) until uniting with their husbands as was the common practice then. Only fallen women/prostitutes did such) so they knew full well that without a man's seed, there would be no children ... and of course they erroneously believed that they should take matters in their own hands to carry on the family lineage.

These daughters knew that "fermented grape juice" would cause a drunken father with no memory of the sexual encounter. Of course these daughters did wrong, in not trusting Jehovah to provide them husbands ... which no doubt He would have done had they not acted so hastily. How the daughters "caused Lot to drink to the point of inebriation" is somewhat of a mystery but it is plain to say that Lot was not, nor ever was a "drunkard". He was a righteous, just, Godly man and monumental shame on those who would paint him otherwise! Lastly there is the accusation against Lot ... "... that Lot failed in reaching his own family to live a righteous life. His sons' in law, and wife perished, and his daughters did wickedly, etc, etc."

To this I answer ... Then Adam failed with Cain and was responsible for him murdering his brother, then Noah was a failure in seeing souls saved after preaching 120 years! NO! The reason that these wicked people did what they did, those in Sodom and all other places is found in Ec. 8:11....

"Because sentence against and evil work is not executed speedily therefore the heart of the sons of men is fully set do evil." (This author notices the hypocrisy of people from other nations who paint America as a "Great Satan" or as a present day "Sodom and Gomorrah", when in reality their own moral climate is much worse than America's! Sad that Christians sit "at ease in America ... enjoying the luxuries here and do not consider that judgment on America for her depravity must surely come in light of that which came on S&G etc.)

Hard Questions For the Skeptics-

1. When Jehovah "appeared" to Abraham did He appear as ... A) One man? B) Two men? C) Three men? Or D) He did not visually appear?

2. Which of the men were addressed as Jehovah? A) The one in the middle? B) On the right? C) On the left? D) All of them?

3. When Abraham saw the three men and he addressed them as Adonai (vs. 3.) Did He address them as, A) your/yourselves plural or, B you/yourself singular (vs4).

4. Is it true in Chapter 18 that 2 times it is recorded, "They said" (the 3 men said) such & such, and the same ("They said") in vs. 5 & 9? True or False

5. If God did appear as a Trinity, i.e. incarnate in 3 human forms, would it be impossible for the three to speak in one voice and as one person speaking? True or False.

6. Can you prove from Genesis 18 & 19 that God appeared to Abraham in the form of one man? Yes or No

7. When Jehovah <u>appeared</u> to and talked with Abraham, IF he appeared "along WITH the three men, then when the Lord was talking to Lot in Ch 19 why was Lot addressing only two men as one in vs.18, i.e. "… not so my Lord.…" plainly singular, and why is there no indication he was talking to someone invisible? To the contrary, Lot was talking to the two *men* /messengers as if they were one, and as well they answered as ONE … as the blessed Lord Jehovah in vs.21-22! So which of the following is correct? (A) God did not really appear to Abraham so also not to Lot. (B) The two men were in-

deed two members of the blessed Trinity and needed to be addressed as one. (C) If that question is answered as is evidenced, the doctrinal truth of the Triune Godhead will be proven. Many will unfortunately say I still don't believe it so that cannot be allowed, just don't confuse me with the facts.

8. Neither Abraham, nor Lot made distinction (when addressing the three or two "men/*angel/* messengers") between the "men" but freely addressed them as one, and as well they (the men) answered to title of Deity in both chapters the reason is as follows. A) They were indeed members of the blessed triune Godhead B) They were only men/created angelic beings on a mission and willingly and readily accepted acclamation of themselves falsely as Deity?

9. How many times in Genesis 18 are 2 of the men called angels i.e. created beings? A) 1 time B) 2 times C) 3 times D) never. (Vs. 22, The two who went to Sodom, were wrongly labeled as 'angels' by the A.V. translation, when they should have been correctly called, 'messengers' <u>sent by the Lord</u>, the other member of the Trinity!) So the correct answer is D so 'never' were they called angels with correct translation. Jehovah did not lie! In verse 21, He said <u>"I" will go down</u> (to Sodom), and so He did go down in the form of two men, i.e. two of the three members of the Trinity who first appeared to

Abraham in verse 2 in the form of men went down to Sodom. The mistaken idea that Jehovah sent two angels/ created beings to Sodom to investigate it makes God/ Jehovah to have falsely spoken when He stood before Abraham. He said "I will go down!" God cannot lie.

10. Is it true an "Angel" or "Angel of the Lord" indeed can be a manifestation of God (Jehovah) Himself in Jewish scriptures as occurred with Hagar, Joshua, Baalam,(with Baalam compare Num.22:35 and 22:38 to identify the "Angel of the Lord" of 22:22), and Gideon (Judges 6, compare 6:12 to 6:16 to identify the Angel of the Lord). A) True? B) False?

11. Is it true that the two '*angels*' who came to visit Lot at Sodom were called "Created Angelic Beings?" A) True B) False.

12. Did the "Angels of the Lord" who visited Lot have supernatural power, i.e. Blinding the wicked, and incinerating the two wicked cities? A) True? B) False

13. Is God able to visibly manifest Himself as 3 Men? A) Yes B) No.

14. If the 2 "Angels of the Lord" in Gen.19 were the same as "Angels (Heb. '*messengers*') of the Lord" who appeared to Hagar, Jacob, Baalam, Joshua, and Gideon then is it wrong to ascribe Deity to them? A) Yes B) No.

15. Is there proof they were not indeed "God" manifested in human form? A) Yes B) No.

16. Since most Christian scholars deny the Trinity appeared to Abraham and Lot, do they have, A) Much support from Genesis 18-19 to support that position, or B) None at all from those chapters since they clearly indicate the contrary.

17. Where did Jehovah state He was going to "send" 2 created angels to scope out the wickedness of Sodom and Gomorrah instead of going Himself? (A) Nowhere in Scripture, in fact He did indeed go down. (B). Nowhere, but He changed His mind about keeping His Word. (C).In Genesis ch. 51?

18. The English word "Angel" never means other than a "created heavenly angelic being" and the Hebrew/Greek text must give way to the English translation. A.) True (as per Ruckmanism) B.) False; the underlying inspired Hebrew/Greek must be honored and reverenced.

19. Since the original Hebrew/Greek Autographs, the original hand written autographed manuscript penned by the original writers of the Hebrew/Greek Old and New Testaments were no doubt worn out or destroyed by the end of the first or second centuries, the world was without the infallible Word of God until King James produced it in 1611 a.d. A) True B) False.

UNHOLY BEINGS

To more clearly understand the truth of "God becoming flesh" one needs to examine the Biblical truth where "fallen angels" become flesh and dwell among us. Angels have and do become flesh (at least while indwelling the host human body) as demonically indwelt men. Men fully developed with their own personalities who fall victim to being/becoming temporarily indwelt by demons with personalities of their own. Thus the same with Jesus – Jesus being born a man with a human personality but being indwelt with (permanently, the difference being) one person of the God Head "The Word".

John 1:1, 14. Notice – Jesus was NOT simply "a man indwelt permanently with God" He was the "only virgin born, begotten Son of God, conceived by the Holy Spirit who was indeed God permanently incarnate in the flesh!" Thus Jesus could and truly can be called God – Jehovah in sinless flesh.

The truth that the reality of demons/demonic forces are real goes without dispute among all who accept the Bible as God's Word no matter what denomination! Cannot these forces be active in subverting and corrupting the Biblical facts by false reasoning and conclusions of religious scholars who are demonically influenced? Are they without possibility of error in their Biblical studies? Are they not subject to demonic "thought" at times? The Apostle Peter was when he accepted Satanic thought and expressed it as his own sentiment. Remember Peter (Matt

16:21,22) took Jesus aside rebuking him. Peter told Jesus that he was wrong in teaching that he was going to suffer & die at the hands of the chief priests & the law be put to death, and raised the 3rd day! So it is no doubt that most Bible commentators (past *and* present) have bowed to demonic anti-Trinitarian sentiments in their approach to Genesis 18.

The idea of God appearing in 3 separate physical anthropomorphic forms to Abraham is repugnant to the common Trinitarian view of God. Two of the Trinity were made manifest in the flesh to Jacob in Gen. 32 in the first of the chapter and then at the end of the chapter one of them wrestled with him. Only one was in human form in the incarnation of God (the Word) — the second person of the Trinity through the womb of the virgin Mary — namely the Lord Jesus Christ! To them, no doubt, it is not a question of whether God could or could not manifest himself in 3 separate anthropomorphic/human type forms in Gen.18, but rather if he would or would not (and most don't believe he did or would)!The simple undisputable facts of Gen 18 (as presented) upholds the truth that the Trinity was manifested in human form! There is absolutely no evidence to speak or teach differently! To add further understanding I bring you to an analogy of the life of Christ and demon possession.

The New Testament in particular plainly teaches that evil disembodied spirits come and go at will, (unless cast out by Jesus) inhabiting the physical body of men, women and children. Following we shall examine closely this indwellment to conclusively, prove that not only was it possible for God to literally come in his personage of the Word to reside in a physical body, but that he did so in the person of Jesus Christ. First it needs be emphasized that demons/ unclean spirits are not an influence such as the wind, rain or other influences in nature. Demons are real and literal spirits with personalities, which have the powers of common mankind including thinking, reasoning, and fear of judgment, intelligence, travel, memory, pain and isolation.

Notice Matt 12:43-45: *43: When the __unclean spirit is gone__ out of a man, he walketh through dry places, seeking rest, and findeth none. 44: Then he saith, __I will return__ into my house from whence I came out; and when he is come, he findeth it empty, swept, and garnished. 45: Then goeth he, and taketh with himself __seven other spirits__ more wicked than himself, and they enter in and dwell there: and the last state of that man is worse than the first. Even so shall it be also unto this wicked generation.* Take note of the following:

1. The demon/unclean spirit was living inside this man. The Demon indwelt that man and lived inside his body. The body of the indwelt man was "host" to the evil spirit. The truth about possession is perfectly set out. Two separate personalities residing in one body: a sinful man and an unclean spirit. Now, if a fallen demon/ disembodied spirit can live inside a physical body then who can possibly say that God himself was incapable of doing the same by literally becoming encased in a body of flesh & bone as He certainly did in the Incarnation of God becoming Christ?

2. (2) Notice verse 43, the demon travels out and away from his "host" body possibly having been "successfully exorcised" or cast out. Perhaps the "host" person had a type of moral restoration. May be he had a personal moral determination to reform/clean up his act, perhaps by church membership, baptism whatever, but the demon left. We who are born again believers know that only by the new birth, conversion, and by the indwelling Holy Spirit, is one able to be permanently delivered from indwelling evil spirits.

3. (3) Next the scripture says the demon returns and overpowers the will of the "host" person to "control" him to his bidding of evil things. The very concept of God himself becoming incarnate easily explains the simple truth that our Lord Jesus Christ had two separate but yet distinct natures but combined as one person. Now this truth is further magnified when one realizes more than one "person"- personages can truly live in one body. Verse 45 tells us that the demon spirit brings along seven other evil personages, or intelligent evil spirit beings with him to re-inhabit the body of the man in question.

Who can deny this? Is this a parable? Not hardly! Even if it were a parable — all, <u>absolutely all,</u> — parables are true, not false stories. They may well have been spoken to convey a different truth, or concept, to teach a lesson. In John 17:1: Jesus prayed ... *the hour is come; glorify thy Son, that thy Son also may glorify thee.* Sadly the Watchtower Society attempts to use this verse, and others similar to it, to ridicule the idea that Jesus is God by saying, "If Jesus really were God then here is a verse (John 17:1) where he is praying to himself. Here the truth of demonic indwellment bears the torch of a higher truth in showing the following: If demons, who have separate and distinct personalities, are able to live in and indwell in the body of a person, who has a personality of his own thus giving that person more than one personality, then how easy it is to conclude that Jesus in John 17 is not praying to himself but rather the man Jesus-the carpenters son, the man Jesus' personality which learned and grew in wisdom and stature — the man Jesus, who had a beginning in the virgin Mary's womb as a normal man, yet without sin, was praying from that same personality to His Father in heaven. At the same time the "God the Word personality" incarnate in Him (the second member of the Trinity) was merely silent!

Jesus, God in the Flesh

Searching the scripture it is easy to see that at times The man Jesus spoke: *"I thirst", " I am tired, " or "I am Hungry"*, or was sweating as it were great drops of blood-this was not the "God" personality - God can not thirst, hunger, etc, then at other times the God personality would speak through him, "Be healed, rise up take thy bed and walk" — He would "know" peoples thoughts and hearts — calm the raging tempest and still the trouble waters! The simple truth of the incarnation by studying demonic indwellment truly shreds the false idea that Jesus Christ could not possibly have been God in the flesh. Indeed he was truly God and truly Man; ie.: two separate and distinct natures in one body, blended as one person.

Matthew 8:28-34: 28: And when he was come to the other side into the country of the Gergesenes, there met him two possessed with devils, coming out of the tombs, exceeding fierce, so that no man might pass by that way. 29: And, behold, they cried out, saying, <u>What have we to do with thee</u>, Jesus, thou Son of God? art thou come hither to torment us before the time? 30: And there was a good way off from them an herd of many swine feeding. 31: So the devils besought him, saying, If thou cast us out, suffer us <u>to go away into the herd of swine.</u> 32: And he said unto them, <u>Go</u>. And when they were come out, they went into the herd of swine: and, behold, the whole herd of swine ran violently down a steep place into the sea, and perished in the waters. 33: And they that kept them fled, and went their ways into the city, and told everything, and what was befallen to the possessed of the devils. 34: And, behold, the whole city came out to meet Jesus: and when they saw him, they besought him that he would depart out of their coasts.

Notice here the two men with these legion demons asked Jesus if he was going to torment them before their time? Again, indisputable truth, to the anti-deity of Christ crowd, that more than one personality can indeed indwell the same body! Even the demons confessed that Jesus was the Son of God, due to his power over them (Matthew 8:29; Mark 4:41).

So did the Prophets! Jesus rebuked the wind, which proves His divine power over the forces of nature (Matthew 14:33). The idea voiced by some Watchtower followers that Jesus just happened to be in the place where the winds suddenly ceased is a rationalization of their own thinking. Mark recognized the deity of Christ in Mark 1:1. Read also Luke 22:70 and Mark 14:61, where Jesus confessed that He is the Son of God. The angel announced before the birth of Jesus that He was to be the Son of God (naturally if "The Son of God" then equal with God). We who are "Sons of God" are not equal to Jesus as is God's Sinless only Begotten Son.

He was the "Only Begotten of God" by His conception by the Holy Ghost and us, being adopted from the sinful family of Adam and being regenerated/transformed by the Spirit of God! Read also John 5:25; 10:36; and 11:4. Jesus claimed that He was the Son of God in Matthew 27:40,43; Mark 14:61,62;

Luke 22:70; John 5:25; 10:36; and 11:4. Jesus possesses the life-giving power of Deity (John 5:21,26; Hebrews 7:16; John 17:3-5; 10:17,18). A final note here must be added. This author by no means is teaching that Jesus was merely a man with the Spirit of God coming and/or going at will but that God had permanently and eternally encased himself in human flesh (i.e. 2 personalities in one, being the only comparison.) in the person of The Lord Jesus Christ. The scripture is clear that God is able to descend/travel to earth to "encase" (incarnate) himself inside a physical body. I Timothy 3:16 expressly states: *And without controversy great is the mystery of godliness:* **_God was manifest in the flesh_**, *justified in the Spirit, seen of angels, preached unto the Gentiles, believed on in the world, received up into glory.* The Apostle John concurs: (John 1:1,14) *In the beginning was the Word, and the Word was with God, and the Word was God....And the Word was made flesh, and dwelt among us.*

Jesus Possessed Divine Attributes

Omnipotence: all powerful (Matthew 28:18; Revelation 1:8; John 17:2; Ephesians 1:20-22). He has power over disease in Luke 4:38-44. He raised Lazarus from the dead in John 11, proving His power over death. He has power over all things, as proved in Hebrews 2:8; 1:3 and Matthew 28:18.

Omniscience: He knows all things (John 16:30; 2:24; Matthew 24; 25 Colossians 2:3; John 4:16-19; 1:48; Mark 2:8).

Omnipresence: He is able to be present everywhere at the same time (Matthew 18:20; 28:20; 1 Corinthians 1:2; Ephesians 1:23).

Next notice 1 John 5:20: _even in his Son Jesus Christ. This is the true God, and eternal life._ How simple therefore to understand that Jesus could "pray to his Father in heaven" and yet be very "God in the flesh! "No! Jesus did not "represent" God in the flesh - He was literally God in the flesh. Notice also Titus 2:13 "Looking for that blessed hope and the glorious appearing of the great God and our Savior! 2 Corinthians 5:19 tells us "To wit God was in Christ reconciling the world unto himself!"

Plainly Jesus was indeed God come in the flesh! Jesus received worship (Matthew 9:18, etc.). Hebrews Chapter l assigns deity to the son before the incarnation took place in eternity past. Jesus had all the credentials of deity — raising the dead, healing the sick of all diseases & infirmaries, reading the hearts & minds of those around him- as well as all angels of God were commanded to worship him and him alone (Hebrews 1:6). He also allowed and accepted human worship (Mt. 2:11; 8:2; 14:33). Only God and God alone is ever to be worshiped! Jesus was truly God who came and was manifested in the flesh!

The Holy Spirit,
Third Person of the Trinity

For there are three that bear record in heaven,
The Father, the Word, and the Holy Ghost:
And these three are one.
1 John 5:17

The Holy Spirit is the third Person of the Trinity. In the Old Testament the Spirit of God is described as the very presence of God displayed. In the New Testament we see the 3rd Person of the Trinity as a separate and unique Person of the Godhead. Look at John 7:33-39, here Christ foretells His death and ascension and it is clearly written that the Holy Ghost would not be "given" until Jesus had been glorified (through His crucifixion & resurrection) ... But this spoke he of the Spirit, which they that believe on him should receive: for the Holy Ghost was not yet given, because that Jesus was not yet glorified, Jn.. 7:39. (Some Christians scoff at the idea of the blessed Holy Spirit taking human form ... but they forget that He did indeed take other forms at will.... In John the form of a dove ... in Acts the form of cloven tongues of fire etc. so why so incredulous are they at His taking form of man in Gen.18?) The same Holy Spirit (very person of God) that indwelt and empowered Jesus Christ to carry out the works of God, is the same Person which lives in every believer today. Jesus said "And He that sent me is with me: The Father hath not left me alone; For I do always those things that please Him." John 8:29.

God is a Spirit (John 4:24) which abided "with" Jesus throughout His life but throughout Jesus' teachings in John Chapters 14-17 He speaks of "another" Comforter which leads us to see there is some other person who shall abide with and is made available to us as believers, as he was available to the followers of Jesus in his days on earth…."I will pray the Father and he shall give you <u>another</u> Comforter, that he may abide with you forever; even the Spirit of truth; whom the world cannot receive, because it seeth him not, neither knoweth him; but ye know him; for He dwelleth with you, and shall <u>be in you</u>. I will not leave you comfortless: I will come to you". Jesus Christ represented God in the flesh just as the Holy Spirit represents Jesus to each believer today. When a person receives Jesus Christ as Lord and Savior then that means the Spirit, which was in Jesus, God's Holy Spirit, will come and reside with the new believer and will give him/her the divine attributes which Jesus displayed, being God in the flesh. (see John 14:26) We also see in 1 Corinthians 3:16,17

Paul writes about the body of the Christian being the "Temple of God" … Know ye not that ye are the temple of God, and that the Spirit of God "dwelleth in you"? When a person becomes saved, the third person of the Trinity lives within that person and any damage, abuse or violation of purity done to the temple of the Holy Spirit is done as unto God himself. Paul writes.... But he that is joined unto the Lord is one Spirit. What? Know ye not that your body is the temple of the Holy Ghost which is in you, which ye have of God, and ye are not your own? For ye are bought with a price: therefore glorify God in your body, and in your spirit, which are God's. (1 Cor. 6:17,19,20). The Holy Ghost is such a vital part of the Trinity being equal with God (from creation) and Jesus (our example of who God is) "<u>He</u>", the Spirit of Truth (Jn 16:13,14) because "<u>He</u>" (person) is the guide into God's truth and ways. As no man has seen God, we can see (identify) God through the works of the Holy Spirit in God's people today, as then. (Amazing the Church readily believes that "Jehovah God ... or The Word Jesus Christ" are scripturally able to manifest themselves physically in physical form, but the Holy Spirit is not able to do the same!)

As we cannot visually see the Trinity with the human eye as no man ever has or will in their actual essence at least in this life, we see that God revealed himself to Abraham that day in Genesis 18 through an anthropomorphic manifestation of three men. May God lead you into his truth through the third person of the Trinity, to know the meaning of the contents of this booklet.... For all the promises of God in him *are* yea, and in him A-men', unto the glory of God by us. Now he which stablisheth us with you in Christ, and hath anointed us is God; who hath also sealed us, and "given the earnest of the Spirit in our hearts. (2 Cor. 1:20-22)

Part VII:
Viewpoints from Other Sources

Then there is Ruckmanism, which claims the King James Version 1611 is superior to the text from which it was taken and that no extant Greek/Hebrew m/s are worthy of being called the true word of God. Ruckmans heresy has split and divided good Christians causing church splits, division, contentions and deep disharmony in the ranks of Bible believing fundamental churches. Ruckmanism makes mockery of using the Hebrew/Greek M.S. in clarifications of difficult texts, such as this present booklet does on Gen. 18-19.

Ryrie in his study Bible notes on Genesis 18, tried to identify the three men as three angels. Apparently the Lord (Trinity) is incapable of transforming themselves into physical bodies, when in fact he easily believes that the second person of the Trinity did, indeed just that, when He as "The Word — Jesus Christ" became flesh (John 1:14). Reading Genesis 18 it is clear that Abraham has no doubt as to whom the three men were when he saw them arrive. This is an important note. If three strange/unknown men walked up to anyone's door (or tent) naturally there would be the question "who are you" and / or "What can I do for you?" How could Abraham therefore instantly recognize these three men as "The triune God revealed physically" and address them as "Adonai" (Remember this title was only for almighty Jehovah).

Simple! Jehovah had already visited Abraham in chapter 17 when he was 99 years old and identified himself as "Almighty God", and now in Chapter 18 no doubt as the same three personage in the flesh! It must be obvious that in Chapter 17 Jehovah appeared in the same fashion to Abraham as "three men". This author has become convinced that satanic and demonic forces & influences have attacked the clear understanding of Genesis 18 Trinity revelation due to their hatred of the doctrine and the truth of the incarnation/deity of the Lord Jesus Christ. Sadly, thus far in believers realm it seems Satan has prevailed in perverting the truth of the Trinity in human form in Genesis 18.

In accomplishing this, the devil therefore can easily use the false premise that the Trinity could not possibly incarnate themselves in human flesh/form in Genesis 18 nor in Jesus Christ as God in the flesh. The next step is obvious in his teaching that "Jesus was indeed God in the flesh but not literally, but as God's representative." The idea that three members of the Trinity manifested themselves in the flesh to Abraham at one time seems repugnant to many Bible teachers, and laymen. This author's simple question is "Why should it be?"

Genesis 18 plainly proves it did occur! We need but to examine only two more manifestations of one member of the Godhead in human form to settle the issue. Perhaps here it would be good to pause to make the following point in light of this skepticism!

God or the Godhead seems to have indicated His basic spiritual form was reflected in His creation of man. Genesis tells us (Genesis 1:26,27) "And God said, Let us make man in our image. ... So God created man in His own image ..." Now to say, as many do, that this image was the spiritual image only i.e. soul & spirit is to side step this issue, especially when God appeared as three men in Genesis 18. Of course, God is not "mortal man" but scripture clearly indicates He (They the Godhead) certainly do or can manifest themselves in human form and that at will. Take the first case of Jacob wrestling the man at night in Genesis 32. Here we see one member of the Trinity wrestling Jacob, appearing as a man but clearly manifested as "God" (Genesis 32:30 & 35:9).

Next, as a warrior man with a sword who identifies himself as "Captain of the host of the Lord" (who appeared to Joshua before the battle of Jericho) who was clearly identified as "The Lord" in Joshua 5:14-6:2. Then finally, as one member of the Trinity who took upon himself the permanent form of man when "The Word - Jesus Christ" became flesh, (John 1:14).

Remember the man, which was wrestling Jacob at night (Genesis 32)? He is later called "The angel (again '*messenger*') of the Lord" in Hosea 12:3,4, but to say that this man was merely an angel (such as created angels) is to degrade the Godhead. Remembering the word "angel" in Hebrew and Greek easily means messenger. Couple this with the fact that each member of the Godhead can operate as liaison for the other two (while in complete agreement with them). It is easy to see how the angel/messenger was in reality one member of the Godhead sent and doing the bidding of the consensus will of all three.

Was not the Lord Jesus Christ 'sent' into the world from his pre-incarnate state to do the bidding of His heavenly Father? Did Jacob look upon this man as a mere 'angel' or created being? Absolutely not! Certainly at first Jacob knew not who this man really was, as evidenced, by reading verse 29 when Jacob (in the midst of the wrestling) said "What is your name?" The man wrestler refused to say. As the night began to dawn toward day, with Jacob refusing to yield to failure, the man/wrestler (yes, incarnate Deity) pronounces a blessing on Jacob. Jacob clearly then recognizes His Deity. Verse 30 tells us, "… and Jacob called the name of the place Peniel (the face of God) for I have seen God face to face and my life is preserved."

Notice in **Isaiah 37:36** that the Angel of the Lord, i.e. Messenger of Jehovah "went forth," i.e…. "Moved or traveled" <u>to</u> the camp of the Assyrians and while traveling to or through that camp put to death 185,000 men! The important notation here is that the Lord did not merely "sit on His throne in the heavens and issue a decree of death thus carried out by the "Word of that Decree" (of course he could have but didn't), but rather a messenger of Jehovah (no doubt one of the other members of the Triune Godhead) "went forth"… "Traveled" to that camp and executed those 185,000 souls **personally!**

This author is pointing out the **parallel** between Jehovah in Gen.18-19, in "sending" two messengers/angels/members of the Godhead **personally** on to Sodom & Gomorrah to destroy it with (the parallel being) the one messenger/angel/member of the Godhead which was **personally** sent to destroy the 185,000. This fortunately further establishes the truth of one or two members of the Triune Godhead in action as messenger/liaison for the other(s) of the Godhead!

These events give us absolute proof that...*THE TERM "ANGEL or MESSENGER" (MALAK 4930 HEBREW) ARE AT TIMES GIVEN TO JEHOVAH THE LORD GOD ADONAI OR/AND PERSONAGES OF THE TRINITY! ALSO THAT:* a) God took an incarnate physical form in shape of man,... b) God was not recognized at first as anything other than a man,... c) God (one personality of the Trinity) physically took form to engage in discourse between himself and man. d) God can certainly physically incarnate himself into the form of man in one, two or three men at will.

Now in recapping the above information which is applicable to:

1. God, as He walked (three or any one of the three) in the garden of Eden in the cool of the day., (Gen 3)

2. God, as He discussed the ark with Noah, (Gen 6)

3. The Lord, as Abraham built an altar unto to the Lord, (Gen. 12:7)

4. The Lord, when He made the promised covenant to Abraham, (Gen. 17)

5. The three men (God incarnate in three personalities) as they had discourse with Abraham over Sodom, (Gen.18.) and then as two men visiting Lot in ch.19 and called "angels".

6. The man (God incarnate) wrestled Jacob, (Gen.32)

7. The Lord appearing to Joshua (as the man with the sword drawn) just before the battle of Jericho (Joshua 5:13-6:5)

The facts stands true that God/Jehovah is a Triune God and has clearly appeared physically as man and interacted with mankind. In closing, the following absolutely infallible conclusions from Gods Holy Word will forever stand!...

1. ... Hebrew ELOHIM (God) is the plural form for God not EL which is singular,

2. ... God said "Let us" make man in our image (plural Genesis 1:26). "Let us go down and confound their language", (Genesis 11:7)

3. ... God appeared in His pluralistic three personage form to Abraham (Genesis Ch 17 & 18) , and with two personages of the Godhead appearing to Lot in ch. 19.

4. ... Jesus Christ is literally God or the second personage in the Triune Godhead, clothed in human flesh"

5. ...That the Lord God Jehovah/Adonai does appear physically (as the Hebrew scriptures plainly show) at times in one, yes and has the option of appearing in ANY ONE of His personages, and is called "The Angel of the Lord"!

Yes it is true an "Angel of the Lord" is a manifestation of God (Jehovah) Himself in Jewish scriptures as occurred with Hagar, Joshua, Balaam,(with Balaam compare Num.22:35 and 22:38 to identify the "Angel of the Lord" of 22:22), and Gideon (Judges 6, compare 6:12 to 6:16 to identify the Angel of the Lord) ... the Hebrew scriptures bear this out as irrefutable fact!

Jesus said, "If ye believe not that I am he, ye shall die in your sins." (John. 8:24). Isaiah 53 speaks plainly of the Messiah. The prophecies given identify Jesus exactly. In fact without exception, every Hebrew prophecy concerning the Messiah clearly identifies the Lord Jesus Christ. I Timothy 3:16 says: "And without controversy, great is the mystery of godliness: ***God was manifest in the flesh, Justified in the Spirit, Seen of Angels, Preached unto the Gentiles, Believed on in the world, Received up into glory.***" Friend, if you reject the Lord Jesus Christ as being God ... "come in the flesh", you will suffer eternal punishment. Turn to Him today, right now, call upon Him and receive Him as your own personal Savior, and He will save you now! The Scriptures tell us, "For whosoever shall call upon the name of the Lord shall be saved." (Romans 10:13)

Old Testament Scriptural Proof
Jehovah Became God In The Flesh

	Compare	With
Christ as Jehovah	Isaiah 40:3	Matthew 3:3
Jehovah of glory	Psalm 24:7, 10	1 Corinthians 2:8; James 2:1
Jehovah our righteousness	Jeremiah 23:5,6	1 Corinthians 1:30
Jehovah above all	Psalm 97:9	John 3:31
Jehovah the first and the last	Isaiah 44:6	Revelation 1:17
Jehovah's equal	Zechariah 13:7	Philippians 2:6
Jehovah of hosts	Isaiah 6: 1-3	John 12:41
Jehovah the Shepherd	Isaiah 40:10,11	Hebrews 13:20
Jehovah the Recipient of Creation	Proverbs 16:4	Colossians 1:16
Jehovah - Messenger of the Covenant	Malachi3:l	Luke 7:27
Jehovah - eternal God and Creator	Psalm 102:24-27	Hebrews 1:8, 10-12
Jehovah - great God and Savior	Hosea 1 :7	1 Corinthians 4:5; 2 Corinthians 5:10; 2 Timothy 4:1
Jehovah - King of Kings and Lord of Lords	Daniel 10: 17	Revelation 1:5; 17:14
Jehovah - Creator of all Things	Isaiah 40:28	John 1:3
Jehovah - Supporter and Preserver of all things	Nehemiah 9:6	Colossians 1:17; Hebrews 1:3

It is this authors sincere prayer that this booklet will bring many souls to a saving knowledge of Jesus Christ as God and King-The second person of the Triune Godhead. Genesis 18 no doubt was meant to be an irrefutable eternal monument to clearly show Jehovah is a Triune God, One God in three persons. For any scholar/theologian or commentator to deny the truth revealed in Genesis 18 is for them to profanely tread on very Holy and Sacred ground. God help the church to see and promote this truth.

THE SINNER'S PRAYER:

Pray the following prayer now, or one similar to it meaning it, and God will save you now and forever:

"Dear Lord Jesus, I come to you as a guilty sinner. I take full responsibility for all my sins. Please, Lord Jesus, have mercy on me and come into my heart right now and save me from all my past, present, and future sins. I accept the payment, in full, you made on the cross for all my sins, past present, and future. I accept you as my God and Savior, please make me born again right now. I believe you died on the cross for my sins and were raised from the dead. Please come into my heart and wash all my sins away in your precious blood. Thank you Lord Jesus. Dear Holy Ghost, Spirit of God, please come into my heart and make me born again right now. I accept you to come into my body and soul and make me the temple of God, the temple of the Holy Ghost. Please was all my sins away in the blood of Jesus Christ, make my heart clean and pure. I accept you as my Comforter, my guide, and my strength. Dear God the Father, I accept your Son Jesus Christ as my God and Savior. I also the free gift of eternal life so I can be born again right now. Thank you Father for the free gift of eternal life. I mean this prayer with all my heart. I love you Lord Jesus. I love you Holy Spirit. I love you Father. In the name of the Father, Son, and Holy Spirit I pray. Amen"

Strong's Exhaustive Concordance of the Bible

Definitions of Hebrew:

0113: Adon (adown) master, sovereign master/owner (rarely used of Jehovah)

0136: Adonay (ad-o-noy) an emphatic form of Lord Jehovah (or God only)

0259: Echad (ekn-awd) united, i.e. one (as an ordinal)

0430; Elohiym (el-o-heem) Gods in the ordinary sense but spec. used (in the plural thus esp.with the art of the supreme God. God (gods).

1376: Gebiyr (gheb-eer) a master-lord

3068: Yhovah (yeh-ho-vaw) self, existent or eternal

4397: Malak (mal-awk)From an unused root meaning to dispatch as a deputy, a sent Messenger of God, an Angel, also a Prophet, Priest or Teacher, Ambassador, King, Messenger.

LASTLY
The Peshitta Aramaic Bible Peshitta Primacy King of All Manuscripts and the Final Word!

SEEMINGLY UNBELIEVABLE! MAGNIFICENT DISCOVERY! THE NEW TESTAMENT IN PRISTINE ORIGINAL TEXT HAS NOW BEEN ESTABLISHED AND CAN BE SCIENTIFICALLY VERIFIED! FOLLOWING ARE AMAZIND FACTS AND SCRIPTURAL BACKGROUND.

1. Jesus our God and Savior promised that His word would be preserved forever. The New Testament was/is just that, "His Word" and must be, and therefore will be kept pure for our use/edification and that being for eternity. Our Lord also said that "…Heaven and earth shall pass away…but my Word endureth forever."

2. The simple fact is that there is no complete Greek N.T. manuscript from the first or second centuries. only portions of such exist. No mirror of the original autographs and 10,000 speculations by the K.J.V. 1611 only sect prove nothing. The oldest complete Greek manuscripts date only from 301-450 A.D.

3. Until now, no one could claim to have a letter perfect copy or reproduction/recreation of the original autographs, since they simply deteriorated out of existence in the first two to four hundred or so years of their creation. they being copied, handled, recopied and passed to the early churches, no doubt soon came to early demise due to frailty, however first and second century copies still exist in the original language of our Lord and his disciples, the Syrian Aramaic (Peshitta)! Absolutely no other language/dialect can make such claim!

The above undeniable facts introduce the ignored/overlooked and maybe even despised by some, first and second century 100% complete Syrian Aramaic Peshitta (Peshitta meaning 'simple/straight') manuscripts which are no doubt exact copies of the original autographs, or possibly copies of original first generation copies of the autographs.

It must be remembered that the autographs were considered by the early church to be sacred, holy, worthy of Divine Honor, and those copyists were no doubt highly fearful of desecrating, corrupting or not copying them exactly as they were written.

So, the following question must be asked. Should the over 2000 Greek New Testament texts called the Textus Receptus or the Received Text (which pretty much mirrors each other, except in some small differences, but still in no way disturbs any of the basic fundamentals of the faith), be used to judge the accuracy of the Peshitta Aramaic manuscripts? Also should those Greek Manuscripts which cannot claim physical unbroken lineage back to the autographs possibly be used to judge each other as to the very minor differences they may have between themselves?

The answer to that is 'absolutely not!' Only those manuscripts which can prove physically unbroken lineage back to the autographs are qualified to do so. The simple language of our Lord Jesus and His disciples was the Aramaic language. Thus the Peshitta Aramaic Scriptures have the physical unbroken lineage back to the originals, and thus are qualified to be judge/ jury/ and executioner/executor to determine the exact text of the original Divine Text and the meaning there of even in the smallest differences!

The question then looms, "How/why have the Greek Manuscripts been exalted above the Aramaic Peshitta? Also, commonly, the question is asked, "How can anyone know for sure that any manuscript, Biblical that is, prove itself to be in itself the exact letter perfect replica of the autographs of the New Testament?" The common answer to that question is, "That it is theologically impossible since the original autographs no longer exist to judge generations of copies made from it."

The solution to that problem is astounding. Enter theologian, David Bauscher who has found computer codes in the now scientifically reestablished Aramaic New Testament. These codes act as a Divine 'watermark' if you will, to prove scientifically that the Aramaic Peshitta New Testament he has translated is a perfect replica of the autographs. He did this by bringing together the majority text (over 200 texts) of the Aramaic Peshitta, comparing them with each other, and discovering the exact number of words in the text which allows computer codes to be revealed! Please visit "David's Store of Bible Translations and Books" visit www.lulu.com/spotlight/gbauscher.

The interesting thing to note is that the codes he discovered, are only found in the Peshitta/Aramaic, and not in the Greek. Here again the fact is reinforced that the original autographs were first written in Aramaic (in the first century), and then within a few days/months translated into the Greek for the Jews of the Diaspora, and other Greek speaking Christians.

One last noteworthy fact. Any atheist/agnostic or infidel can now be shown scientifically/irrefutably that the Peshitta Aramaic New Testament with its verifiable codes could only have been created by our omniscient God and Savior, the Lord Jesus Christ who would have all men to be saved and come to the knowledge of the truth.

We who love the Word of God can also thank God that the Peter Ruckman gigantic heresy (his followers called Ruckmanknights) that the 1611 K.J.V is superior to the manuscripts from which it was taken because it was supposedly Divinely superintended by God (?!), can now be relegated to the dust bin list of heresies long afflicting the church. The Peshitta Aramaic totally blows his false teachings out of the water.

Friend, if this booklet has helped you find salvation please write us today Please tell us your story. Eternity Publications 1252 Sessions Rd. Elgin, SC 29045 (Final revised 12/2/19)

CPSIA information can be obtained
at www.ICGtesting.com
Printed in the USA
FSHW010839200521
81560FS